Guitar Signature Licks

The Best of Eric Clapton
A STEP-BY-STEP BREAKDOWN OF HIS PLAYING TECHNIQUE

BY JEFF PERRIN

Page	Title
2	Introduction
72	AFTER MIDNIGHT
35	BADGE
75	BEFORE YOU ACCUSE ME (TAKE A LOOK AT YOURSELF)
51	COCAINE
46	CROSSROADS (CROSS ROAD BLUES)
14	HAVE YOU EVER LOVED A WOMAN
40	I SHOT THE SHERIFF
41	KNOCKIN' ON HEAVEN'S DOOR
63	LAY DOWN SALLY
3	LAYLA
75	LAYLA (ACOUSTIC VERSION)
43	LITTLE WING
83	PRETENDING
29	THE SUNSHINE OF YOUR LOVE
77	TEARS IN HEAVEN
23	WHITE ROOM
56	WONDERFUL TONIGHT
88	Guitar Notation Legend

This publication is not for sale in the E.C. and/or Australia or New Zealand.

Cover photo by Jeffrey Mayer

ISBN 0-7935-5801-8

7777 W. BLUEMOUND RD. P.O. BOX 13819 MILWAUKEE, WI 53213

Copyright © 1996 by HAL LEONARD CORPORATION
International Copyright Secured   All Rights Reserved

For all works contained herein:
Unauthorized copying, arranging, adapting, recording or public performance is an infringement of copyright.
Infringers are liable under the law.

INTRODUCTION

As one of music's greatest living legends, Eric Clapton has earned himself a distinguished place in music history. With a successful career spanning over three decades, Clapton's influence can be heard in more than one generation of musicians and is present in even the youngest of today's guitarists. Moreover, the appreciation of Eric Clapton's fans not only knows no age limit, it knows no stylistic boundaries as well. Clapton is often cited in magazine interviews as a significant musical influence among guitarists of various styles, ranging from blues to rock to even heavy metal.

While the scope of Clapton's influence upon modern music is certainly well worth a thorough review, the focus of this book is to examine and discuss a more specific (and arguably important) topic, his *music*. With virtually scores of books written about Eric Clapton's career and past musical endeavors, one would be hard-pressed to find a publication that specifically studies Clapton's music from the guitarist's perspective. This book attempts to fill that void by focusing on some of Eric Clapton's most popular songs in a way that helps the beginning to intermediate guitarist explore and learn from some of Eric's finest music.

The Best Of Eric Clapton-Signature Licks book, along with the accompanying recording, effectively serves as a hands-on learning tool with which to study and examine some of Eric Clapton's best music. The book features transcription excerpts from twelve songs that cover an extensive span of Eric Clapton's lengthy career. (Many of the songs covered in the book may be found on the two compilation CDs: *Strange Brew: The Very Best Of Cream*, and *Timepieces: The Best Of Eric Clapton*.) The transcription excerpts showcase some of the more significant and memorable riffs and solos from each of these songs, and include performance notes to help the reader study each example. All of the excerpts also appear in audio form on the book's accompanying CD/cassette recording. This not only lets you hear the guitar in context, but also allows you to more effectively practice the guitar parts in an ensemble setting.

For optimum study, the lead or main guitar part is featured in the right channel while the rhythm section dominates the left channel. With this setup, you may choose to study the examples in the book by:

1. playing along with the recording "as is" in order to hear the riff in context;

2 panning the stereo's balance to the right in order to more clearly hear the featured guitar part; or

3. panning the stereo's balance to the left to allow for rehearsal with just the rhythm section.

By taking full advantage of the described study methods, you should easily be able to learn the songs and prepare them for performance.

Editorial Note:

The Best Of Eric Clapton-Signature Licks book and recording are primarily designed to help you learn and prepare selected Eric Clapton songs for live performance. A more detailed analysis of the theory and techniques involved in many of these songs can be found in the *Eric Clapton-Guitar School* book, also available from Hal Leonard.

LAYLA
(Derek and the Dominoes)
Words and Music by Eric Clapton and Jim Gordon

Example 1 – Introduction

As one of the most celebrated and energetic songs ever recorded by Clapton, "Layla" highlights Eric's tenure as lead guitarist and chief songwriter for his group, Derek and the Dominoes.

Upon first glance of the transcription excerpts for Example 1, you'll notice that there are actually three different guitars performing the song's introduction. In addition, four bars into the tune, *two more* slide guitars enter the picture for a total of *five* different guitar parts (not to mention the additional parts labeled Fills 1 and 2)! This multitude of parts is the result of Eric Clapton's exploitation of the modern recording studio's ability to allow guitarists to "overdub," or layer, multiple guitar parts onto rhythm tracks. While highly effective in creating the illusion of a large orchestra of guitars, this recording method may present a dilemma when it comes time to perform the piece live on stage! Consequently, when approaching this tune for live performance, you'll need to "whittle-down" the arrangement and select the guitar parts from "Layla" which will best accommodate your own musical situation, just as Clapton did. (You don't really think Eric hauled 5-6 extra guitarists on tour just for the sake of one song, do you?)

If you will be performing "Layla" with another guitarist, the most logical choice for arrangement would be to have one guitarist perform the chord riff shown in the bottom staff of the system (Gtr. 3), while the other guitarist performs the lead melody part (labeled Gtr. 1). Obviously, the more guitar players available the better (but not always), as you'll be able to include some of the other guitar parts.

If you're the only guitar player available, you'll need to employ a bit of creative arranging. For example, you could begin the first four bars with the chordal riff played by Gtr. 3 and then switch to the lead melody part (Gtr. 1) when going into measure 5. As this is the point when the rest of the band should join in, the bass player could modify his bass line to make up for the missing chord riff. This is only one of many options, and exactly how you approach your own performance of the song depends on your band's instrumentation as well as your own personal judgment.

Additional note—when performing any of the guitar parts in Example 1, be sure to observe any slurs that appear in the transcription. Appearing as arched lines above notes in the staff and tablature, *slurs* indicate the use of legato (fluid sounding) techniques such as hammer-ons, pull-offs, and slides. (See the notation legend for a specific definition of each slur.) Observing the slurs will help you to best re-create the feel of each riff as heard on the original recording.

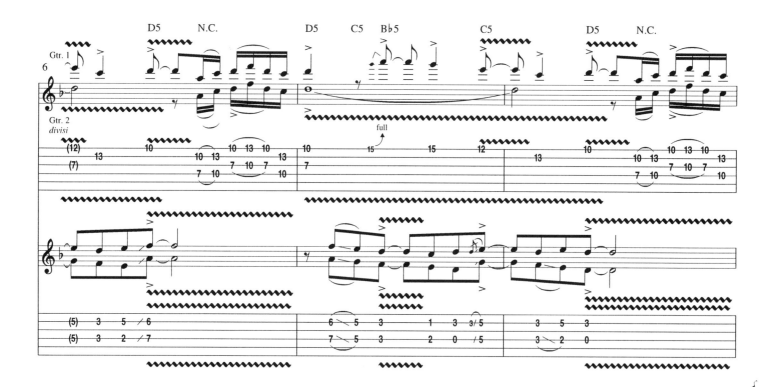
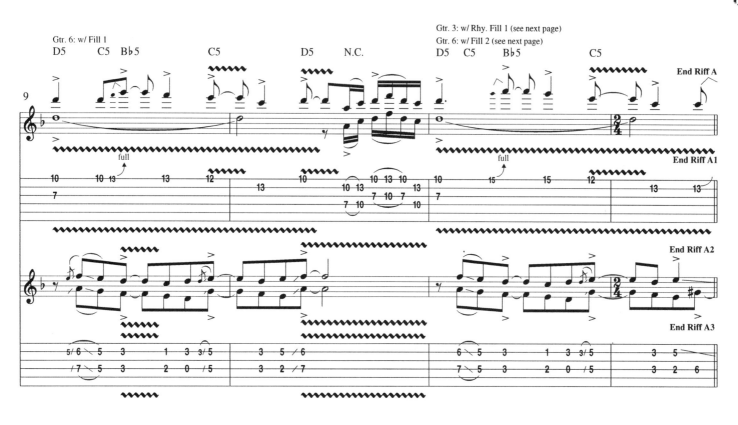

Example 2 – 1st Verse

In the verse sections of "Layla," Eric Clapton uses a simple and effective technique known as *left-hand muting*, in order to give his rhythm playing a funky, aggressive quality. Left-hand muting is a maneuver that involves loosening your hand's grip on a note or chord just enough so that the string(s) stop vibrating. Xs in the staff and tablature indicate where Clapton strums over these muted strings in order to produce a hollow, percussive "chucka-chucka" sound.

To perform left-hand muting on the appropriate chords (chords preceding a rest or muted strum) throughout Example 2, release your left hand's finger pressure off the frets *immediately* after each pick attack. Be careful not to let go of the strings completely after each mute, as you might accidentally sound some open strings.

Another tricky aspect to performing the rhythm guitar part in Example 2 is synching-up the right hand's strumming with the left-hand mutes. The best way to coordinate both hands can be achieved by employing an alternate strumming method sometimes referred to as *pendulum strumming*. This strumming action involves a constant down-up, down-up motion where downstrokes consistently fall on the downbeats, while upstrokes occur on upbeats. For those of you who are not sure how to figure out where the downbeats and upbeats are among the 16th-note rhythms, I've provided some strumming prompts below the tablature in the first few bars. After you've studied the strumming prompts, you'll soon realize that when performing the pendulum strumming in "Layla," you continue the quick strumming motion even during rests or chords held longer than an 8th or 16th note. During these instances (such as in the middle of beat 1, measure 2), the right hand simply passes over the strings silently. (These "silent strums" are indicated in the strumming prompts by parentheses.)

When learning the rhythm guitar part in Example 2, go slowly and take your time. By initially working with the music this way, you'll be able to more easily hear and correct any mistakes in your playing. (Besides, you can't expect to be able to play along with the recording comfortably if you can't even perform the music at a slow tempo.) Have patience. Working with the music in Example 2 will not only help you play the verse section to "Layla" accurately, but it will also teach you the valuable playing techniques found within the music. While you may eventually forget how to play this tune, the knowledge and skills you acquired while learning it will always be with you.

Example 3 - Slide Guitar Solo

The solo in "Layla" serves as a great primer for beginning *slide guitar* playing. However, before you attempt to play with a slide (either metal or glass), first take a look at your guitar. In order to play slide effectively, the action (height) of your strings should be set a little higher than you'd normally have for rock and roll guitar playing. Otherwise, your strings will buzz and the slide will clack annoyingly against the fretboard. (Unless you have experience in setting up guitars, I would suggest borrowing a guitar with higher action for now. If you develop a real yearning for slide guitar, you can always take it to your local repair shop for an adjustment.)

The first thing beginning slide players will need to do is choose a finger on which to place the slide. Try it out on your middle, ring, and pinky fingers individually. (We'll leave the index finger free for muting, as discussed below.) While comfort is a key factor (you don't want the slide to wobble around on your finger too much!), be aware that a lot of players wear the slide on their ring or pinky fingers. This leaves the other digits available for conventional fretting of some basic chords.

When playing through Example 3, you may notice that in order to make the notes sound in tune, you'll need to play them with the slide placed directly over the frets, rather than behind, as you would with the normal fretting approach. Apply just enough pressure on the strings to sound each note with a minimal amount of buzz. (You don't want the slide to come in contact with the fretboard.) If you experience an unusual amount of noise coming from the other strings, try lightly resting your index finger across the strings behind the slide. This muting technique should help quiet things down a bit.

Once you've gotten these basics down, the most difficult part to performing Example 3 will most likely be moving from note to note accurately and cleanly. You'll probably find that it is all too easy to undershoot or overshoot a note while sliding up the fretboard! Take it slowly, and concentrate on hitting the frets themselves, rather than the spaces between them. It may take some time to get used to fretting notes this way, but, after a bit of practice, you may find that playing with a slide is actually not too difficult and is a great device for soloing in the blues-rock idiom.

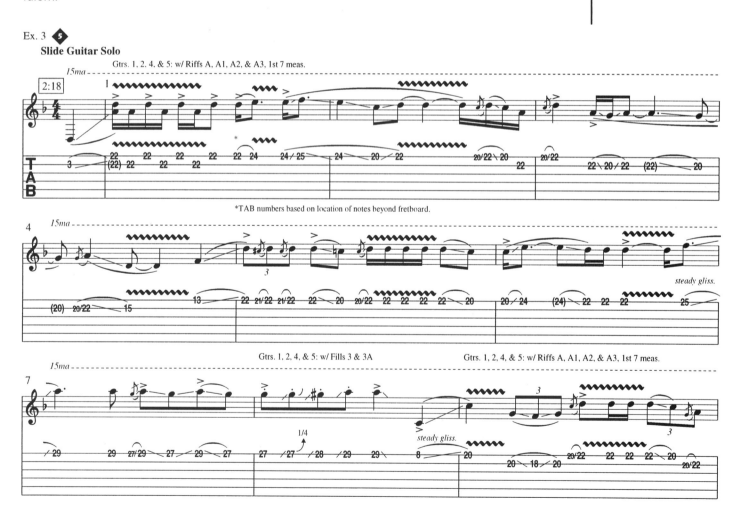

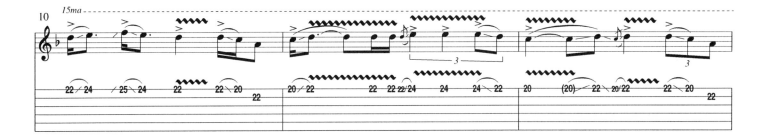

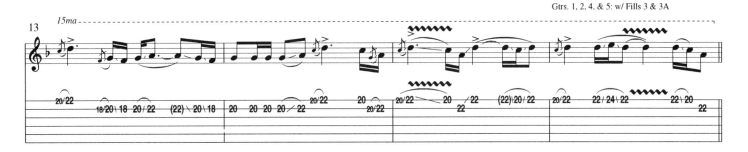

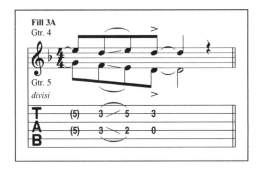

Example 4 - Interlude

When performing Example 4, you can best simulate the sound of the piano's attack by using right-hand *fingerpicking* techniques. This is because when you play a chord on a piano, your fingers usually strike all the keys at the same time, sounding all of the notes of the chord simultaneously. However, when a guitarist strums a chord, he is really moving the pick across the strings and actually picking them in succession. The pick can make contact with only one string at a time, no matter how fast you strum! By using fingerpicking throughout Example 4, you can more closely emulate the sound of the keyboard.

When fingerpicking chords in Example 4, assign each of your right hand's fingers to a specific string during each chord change. For example, when fingerpicking the C chord throughout the first measure, use your pinky finger for the high E string, your ring finger on the 2nd string, and so on. While finger choice is not that much of an issue here (there is a note for each finger), when fingerpicking chords that contain less than five notes, a good rule of thumb ('scuse the pun) is to arrange your fingers so that your thumb plucks the root, or bottom note, of each chord. You'll probably find that this method will provide for the most comfortable fingerpicking options. Whichever digits you choose to fingerpick with, be sure to keep your fingers stationed at their designated strings throughout each chord. This will help you to more comfortably play the chord progression and reduce the chance of your right hand fumbling around in search of the correct strings to pluck.

PENTATONIC SCALE POSITIONS

Perhaps one of the most recognized traits in Eric Clapton's music is his highly emotional lead guitar playing. While some of Eric's most amazing solos can be heard in his earlier work with the rock band Cream (the highly acclaimed solos in "Crossroads," for example), it was through his group Derek and the Dominoes that Clapton took the opportunity to relive and explore his true roots—the blues.

For soloing, Clapton primarily relied on pentatonic major and pentatonic minor scales. (For simplicity's sake, we'll mainly discuss the more frequently used of the two, the minor pentatonic scale. A more thorough discussion of pentatonic scale theory can be found in the *Eric Clapton–Guitar School* book.) The minor pentatonic scale (scale degrees 1, ♭3, 4, 5, ♭7) actually consists of only five (penta) notes (tonic) borrowed from the natural minor scale. This is often the scale of choice for lead guitarists, not just because of its unique bluesy quality, but because the box shape it resembles makes it easy to memorize and play. Shown below are five common pentatonic 'box' patterns, and their positions on the fretboard for the key of A minor. Notice how the patterns "stack" on top of one another up the fretboard. Pattern 1 connects to the top of pattern 2, pattern 2 connects to the top of pattern 3, 3 to the top of 4, 4 to 5, and pattern 5 connects to the top of pattern 1, located one octave (12 frets) above its original position. Learning how the patterns connect to and relate with one another will help you be able to play the blues scale all over the neck in any key.

As noted, the circled notes indicate the root (the note A) in each scale position. To change keys, simply move the patterns up or down the fretboard like a conveyor belt, matching the circled notes to that of the new key. For example, to change to the key of F♯ minor, move the A minor pentatonic pattern 1 down to the 2nd fret (the circled note on the 6th string is the note F♯). All the other pentatonic patterns follow the first one down the three-fret distance as well.

When first learning to play lead guitar, it is often helpful to memorize these blues 'box' patterns and how they relate to each other in several keys. They serve as a great springboard for licks and are excellent "road signs" for making your way around the fretboard. However, all too often beginning guitarists fall into the trap of letting their fingers wander aimlessly around these fretboard shapes when it comes time to solo. While the boxes are great for getting started, be careful not to become so dependent on them that you forget what making music is really about. Ultimately, it should be your ear that tells your fingers how to make the music, and not a set pattern of notes or predetermined licks. Think about this: when Clapton plays, his solo licks and melodies fall into, not out of, these pentatonic shapes!

Minor Pentatonic Scale Positions
(in the key of Am)

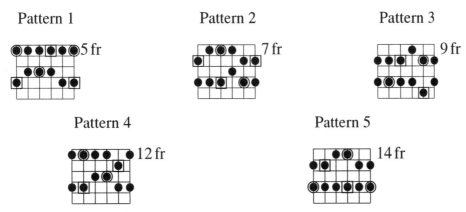

– circled notes are scale roots (the note A)
– notes in squares show the roots (the note C) for the relative major pentatonic scales within each pattern

The following examples are some classic Clapton blues licks similar to those found throughout "Have You Ever Loved a Woman" and other blues songs.

Example 1 – Pattern 1

As you can see, each pattern shape presents its own unique arrangement of notes for one to play with and exploit. As solo skills begin to develop, however, it's not uncommon for guitarists to find themselves gravitating towards a pattern shape or two with which he feels most comfortable. Clapton was no exception. A close study of the transcriptions throughout this book will reveal that Eric played most of his solo licks in the ever-popular pentatonic scale position shown here as pattern 1.

Example 1 shows two different variations of a lick similar to one found in "Have You Ever Loved a Woman" where Clapton repeatedly employs a double stop (two notes played together) with an *oblique bend* to create a catchy, memorable lead "hook." This lick is actually a variation on a common blues riff legendary guitarist Chuck Berry made famous in the intro to his classic hit, "Johnny B. Goode."

When performing these licks, barre your index finger across the 1st and 2nd strings behind the 5th fret and push the 7th string with your ring finger. If you find that you have trouble controlling the bend, or the string tends to slip under your ring finger, try adding the middle finger for support. This should give you the extra "muscle" needed to perform the bend comfortably, especially in the second variation where the bend is held throughout each beat.

Ex. 1
Minor Pent. Pattern 1

Example 2 – Pattern 2

The riff in Example 2 shows how Eric comes up with some cool blues licks using Pattern 2.

When performing the example, use your *ring finger* to slide from the G to A note in the first measure. This will help set your left hand up to more easily play the licks in the following beats. Otherwise, you may find yourself shifting your hand up and down the fretboard unnecessarily, resulting in slightly choppier-sounding rhythms.

To get through the lick in the first two beats of the second bar, use an index finger barre across the 8th fret while your ring finger hammers on the A note at the 10th fret (2nd string).

Ex. 2
Minor Pent. Pattern 2

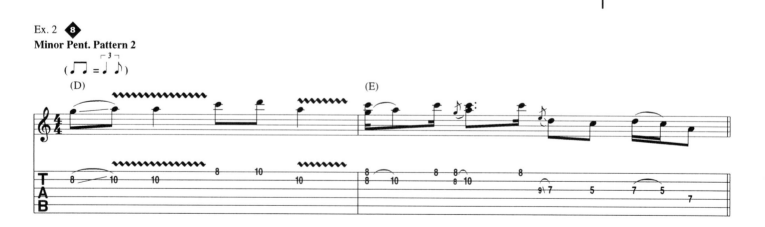

Example 3 – Pattern 4

This final example shows us a fairly simple blues melody played within pentatonic pattern #4.

Ex. 3
Minor Pent. Pattern 4

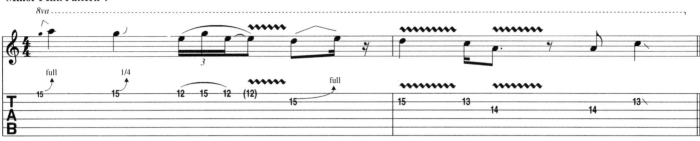

HAVE YOU EVER LOVED A WOMAN
(Derek and the Dominoes)
Words and Music by Billy Myles

Example 1 – Intro Guitar Solo

    "Have You Ever Loved a Woman" provides a great opportunity for you to explore traditional blues guitar, the true foundation of Clapton's playing style. (Note: While Clapton's work with Cream actually preceded the music he made in Derek and the Dominoes, I believe Eric's playing in D.A.T.D. best reflects the early blues influences that ultimately shaped his playing style for years to come.)

    If you're just learning to solo with the blues 'box' patterns discussed earlier, a good exercise for you would be to go through "Have You Ever Loved a Woman" and try to figure out which patterns his licks fit into. For example, the licks in bars 1-2 easily fall in pattern 1, which is located at the 8th fret. (You may recognize the Chuck Berry-style lick in measure 1 from Example 1 of the previous lesson.) Remember, we're in the key of C minor now, so pay attention to the root notes of each pattern.

    By analyzing Clapton's solos this way, you'll not only gain a better understanding of his playing style, but may even be inspired to come up with some similar lead licks of your own!

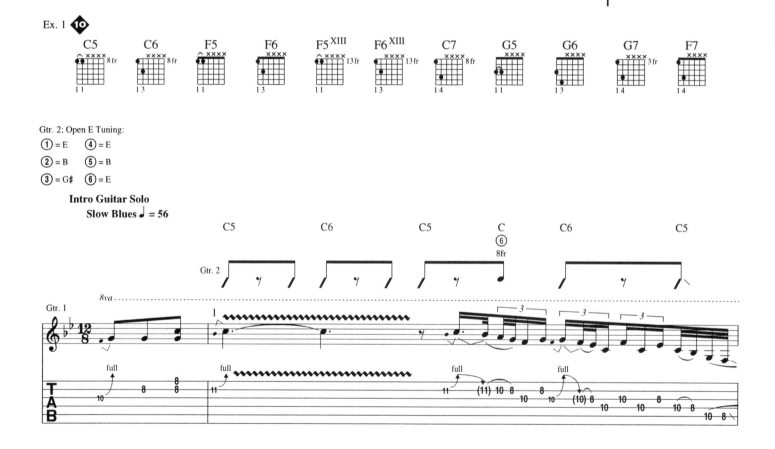

Copyright © 1960 Fort Knox Music, Inc. and Trio Music Co., Inc.
Copyright Renewed
International Copyright Secured   All Rights Reserved   Used by Permission

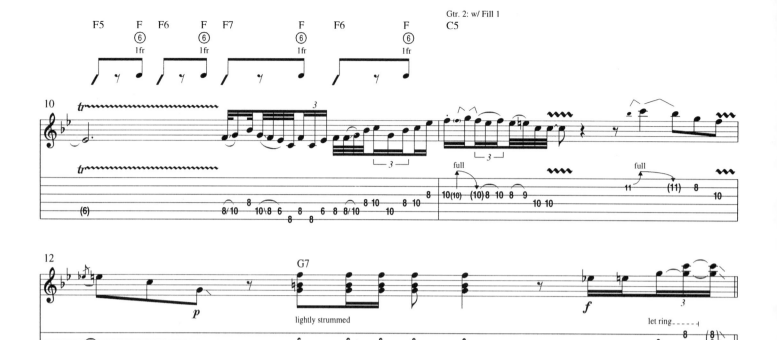

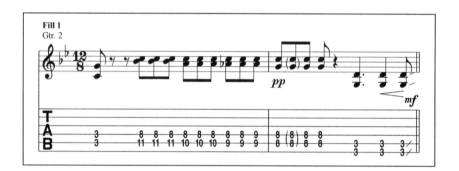

Example 2 – 1st Verse

With second guitarist Duane Allman handling rhythm guitar duties during the verse sections, Eric is free to fill the gaps between vocal lines with wailing blues licks that cry out in support of the moody quality of the song.

Some of the licks in this excerpt serve as great examples of how Clapton often employs *finger vibrato* in order to breathe extra life into key notes in his licks. (Check out the C note found on the 13th fret in the middle of bar 4.) Recreating this wide style of vibrato (sometimes called "bee sting" vibrato) requires that you pivot your entire wrist while rapidly pulling the string downward and releasing it. (Blues legend B. B. King provides a great visual demonstration of this technique, as King's fingers fan out and seemingly wave at the audience whenever he applies this type of vibrato.) Note that while bee sting vibrato is great for making certain notes come alive with emotion, this technique can only be applied to the 2nd-6th strings. As pulling the 1st string downward might yank it completely off the fretboard, you'll need to *push* the note in towards the middle strings instead.

Applying vibrato to a bent note, such as on the note B (11th fret, 2nd string) in measure 11, involves quickly and repeatedly releasing and rebending the note in a steady, even rhythm. This type of vibrato, known as *bend vibrato,* differs from bee sting vibrato in that the pitch fluctuates downward instead of upward. If you experience intonation trouble when performing bend vibrato, you may be overshooting or undershooting your target pitch for the bend. Try practicing the vibrato at a slower rate (the speed at which you bend and release the note) in order to better hear the change in pitch. You'll then be able to more easily make adjustments and train your fingers to apply just the right amount of pressure for each bend. If you still have trouble controlling the pitch of the bend, try adding another finger for support. This reinforced fingering (see Example 1, in the pentatonic pattern lessons) should help to provide the extra finger strength needed to push the string and control the pitch and rhythm of the bend vibrato.

When done properly, bend vibrato can produce a singing, vocal-like quality to a note, making it more noticeable to the audience.

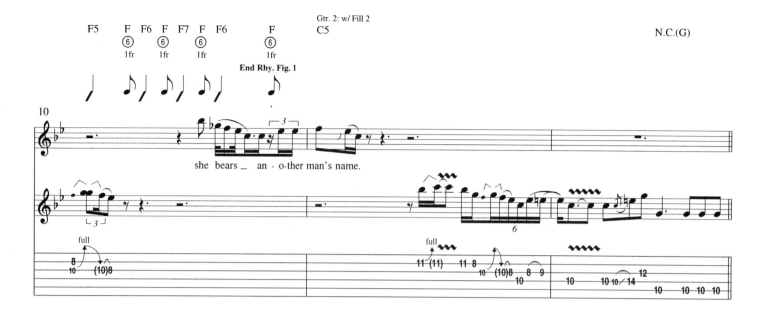

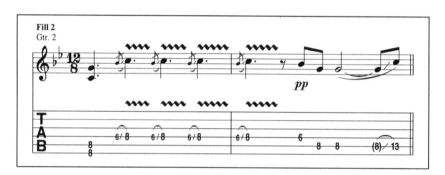

Example 3 – Guitar Solo 1

   Example 3, an excerpt from Duane Allman's solo, showcases some great rhythm accompaniment on the part of Eric Clapton. (Note: Duane's solo is not included on the *Signature Licks* recording in order to allow for more intensive exploration of Clapton's rhythm playing. We'll save discussing Duane Allman's amazing guitar talents for another book!)
   If you've ever found yourself playing back-up guitar at a jam session where the other guitarist enjoyed taking 15-20 minute solos, then you'll really appreciate the comping ideas Eric has to offer in the first four measures of Example 3! Involving much more than simply strumming the same old chord bar after bar, Eric plays lively single-note melody lines and cool sounding double-stop riffs to create an interesting, yet unobtrusive backup rhythm guitar part. When choosing to follow Clapton's footsteps down this avenue of guitar playing, remember these guidelines that can be observed throughout this example:

1. Make sure your rhythm playing stays fairly simple and always supports the feel set by the entire rhythm section. While Clapton did incorporate some solo-type fills into his rhythm part, a majority of his playing here supports the 8th-note pulse established by the rest of the rhythm section.

2. If you do try to include some single-note ideas in your comping, make sure your melodies stay out of the same register as the soloist in order to avoid a dissonant clash of melodies. Notice how most of the pitches in Clapton's "non-chordal" rhythm playing are located in a fairly low to medium note region of the guitar. He makes sure to steer clear of Duane Allman's piercing solo melodies played in the upper register of the guitar.

3. Remember the old saying: "Sometimes less is more." In bars 5-9, we can see that Eric lays back a bit with some ordinary comping in order to give Duane's solo plenty of "breathing space."

By experimenting with and exploring the rhythm guitar playing in "Have You Ever Loved a Woman," you should be able to come up with some cool comping ideas of your own that will help get you through your next 30-minute jam session on "Red House" without falling asleep at the guitar!

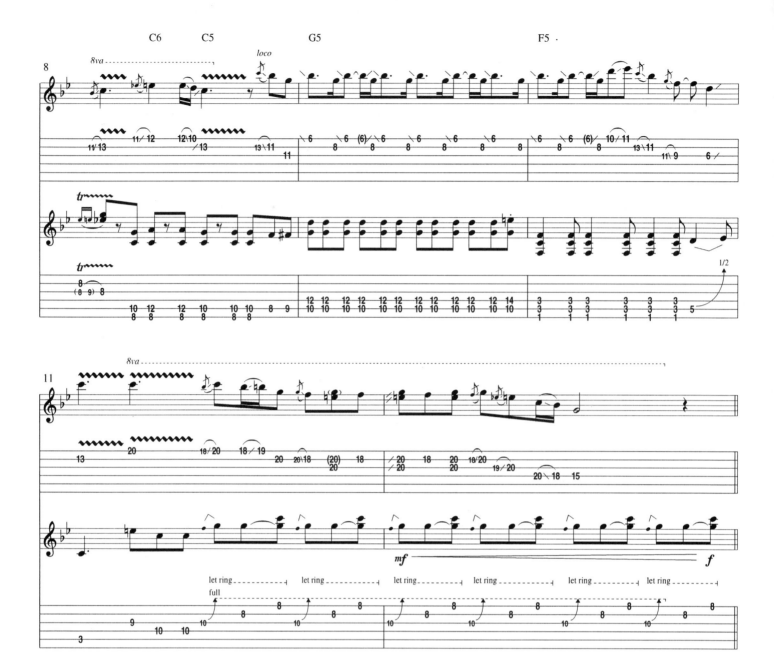

Example 4 – Guitar Solo 2

    The solo in "Have You Ever Loved a Woman" captures some of Clapton's best hard-core blues lead playing to date. Full of tasteful passages laden with an arsenal of useful soloing techniques, one would have nothing to lose from learning this entire excerpt note-for-note! If you're up to the challenge, here are a few tips on learning this and other songs and solos note-for-note:

1. First, go through the transcription to get a general feel for the solo and for what areas of the guitar you'll be working in (just like you did in Example 1 for this tune).

2. Use your ears! To learn the proper rhythms, refer to your CD or tape player often (especially if you don't know how to read standard notation). Listening to the original recording will ultimately give you the best advice on how to play a particular lick.

3. If you find the length or complexity of the solo a little intimidating, begin by working on small groups of notes that you can more easily manage. Break the solo up into smaller, more "chewable" pieces. Some phrases may be consumed several bars at a time, while other licks may need to be nibbled at note-by-note. However, whether you're working on learning the entire solo or just a few licks, start out slowly, and

don't try to play the licks up to speed until you've memorized most of the passage. You'll then be able to focus your concentration on the guitar, rather than the sheet music.

Ex. 4 🔵 13

Guitar Solo 2 (Eric Clapton)

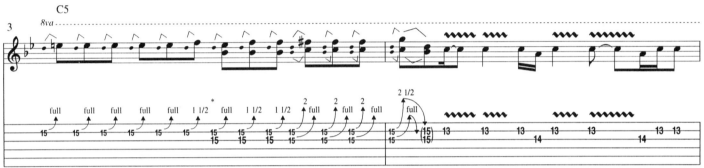

*3rd string caught under finger; not audible on *Signature Licks* recording.

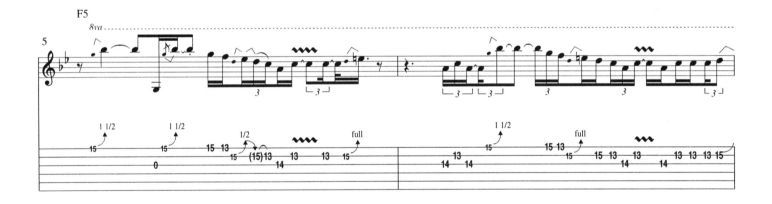

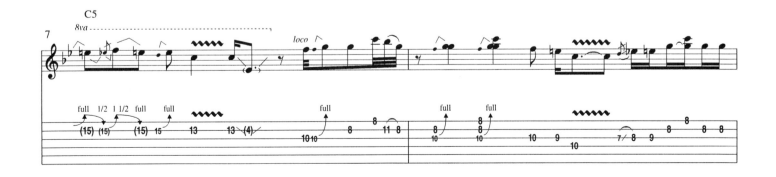

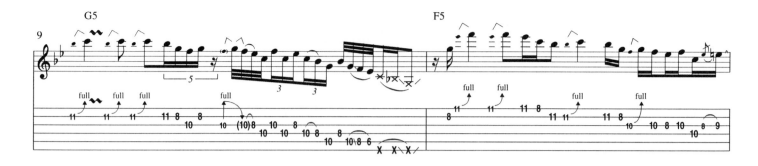
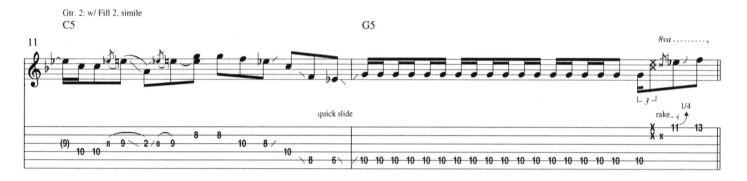

WHITE ROOM
(Cream)
Words and Music by Jack Bruce and Pete Brown

Example 1 – Introduction

In the grand opening to "White Room," Eric Clapton records three separate guitar parts in order to create some lavish-sounding harmonies with the vocals. With a little creative arranging, you can perform all three parts on one guitar. For example, to play all the notes in the first two measures, simply use your index finger to fret the top note, D (10th fret, 1st string), your middle finger to fret the next note down, B♭ (11th fret, 2nd string), and your ring finger on the bottom note, G (12th fret, 3rd string). While this triad should be fairly easy to manage, the harmony parts in bars 3-4 will require some of the creative arranging skills I mentioned earlier. To perform these three solo parts together, use your middle and index fingers to fret the top two notes, A (10th fret, 2nd string) and F (10th fret, 3rd string), respectively. However, you'll need to move the D note in the bottom staff from the 7th fret to the 12th fret on the 4th string! (Obviously, you can't play the F and D notes together because they both appear on the same string!) For the harmonies in bar 4, your index finger plays the G note at the 8th fret on the 2nd string, and the middle and ring fingers fret the remaining notes in a fashion similar to the triad found in measure 1. Observe that this relocates the C note (3rd string) in the bottom staff from the 5th fret to the 10th fret on the 4th string. While holding all three notes, you can then perform the hammer-on/pull-off from C (10th fret, 4th string) to D (12th fret) with your pinky finger. When playing through measures 5-9, you can employ the same left-hand fingering positions that you used throughout the first four bars.

Whenever you encounter a similar situation involving multiple guitar parts, try exploring new fret positions to see if the music can be effectively arranged for a single instrument. Rather than just a means of learning solos note-for-note, this type of creative thinking helps enlighten your knowledge of the guitar's fretboard and educates you on the many positions available for a single note or chord.

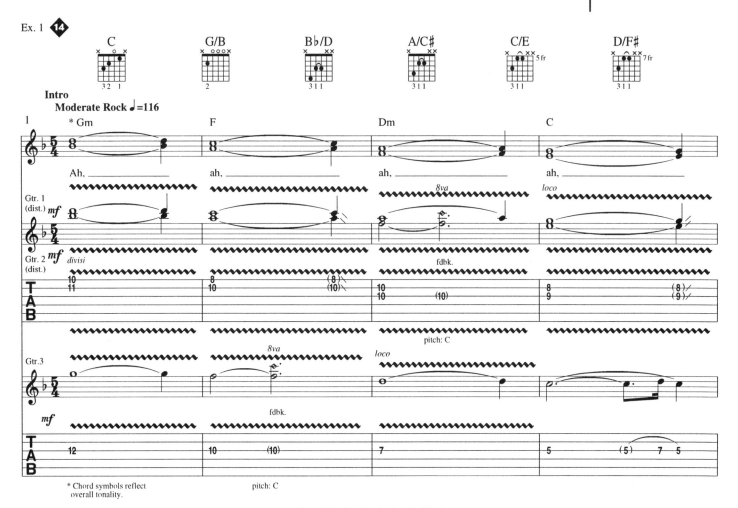

Copyright © 1968 by Dratleaf Ltd.
All Rights Administered by Unichappell Music Inc.
International Copyright Secured   All Rights Reserved

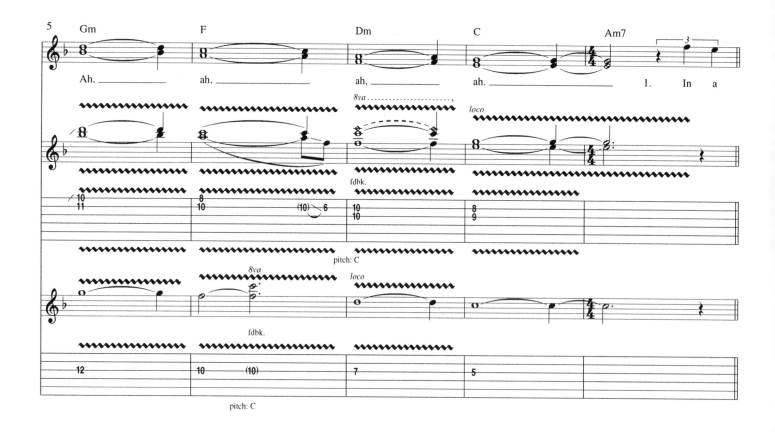

Example 2 – 1st Verse

The first four bars of Example 2 comprise the now-classic riff that makes up the verse section to "White Room." Here we can see that Clapton used several open chords to give his guitar tracks a bright, shimmering quality. This is because the open strings used with open chords generally produce a brighter timbre than that of fretted notes.

When playing through the C5, G/B, and Csus2 open chords, be sure to give the notes in each chord the appropriate sustain by observing the term "let ring—" in the transcription. This is important in re-creating the original feel of the guitar part, as it allows for the root of each chord to sound with all the other notes played.

Example 3 – Bridge

During this serene bridge section to "White Room," Clapton employs the use of a wah-wah pedal to liven up some otherwise ordinary-sounding guitar chords. For those of you unfamiliar with this device, a *wah-wah* is a foot pedal that rocks back and forth, dramatically altering the guitar's sound between a bass and treble tone. When used to the extreme, as Clapton does in "White Room," the pedal can produce a dramatic, vocal-like effect on the guitar. In the transcription, rhythm slashes above the staff roughly show just how Clapton applies his pedal to produce the effect you hear on the original recording. As indicated in the sheet music, Xs show when the pedal is in the down position, while Os represent when it's in the up position. However, if you have such an effective pedal, your best bet in re-creating Clapton's wah usage would be to listen to the original recording and try to imitate the wah's sound by ear. (The effect on the recording varies too much to be accurately caught on paper in such limited space.)

Example 4 – Outro Guitar Solo

Perhaps the most ear-catching licks in the outro to "White Room" are the repetitive series of 16th notes beginning in measure 7 and continuing through the first three beats of measure 8. To best play through these measures, use an index finger barre across the 1st and 2nd strings at the 13th fret. This will cut down on any unnecessary left-hand movement and help produce cleaner-sounding notes. You can also ensure smoother rhythms by employing a down-pick attack on the C note (13th fret, 2nd string) for each hammer-on technique and an up-pick for every F note (13th fret, 1st string). Similarly reappearing in other solos, this stirring lick can definitely be considered one of Eric Clapton's signature licks!

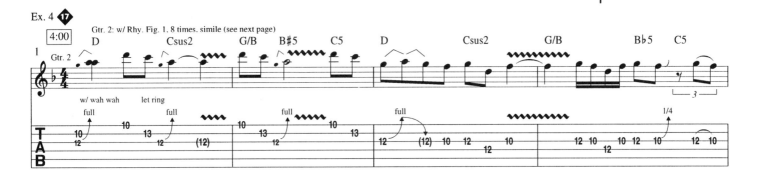

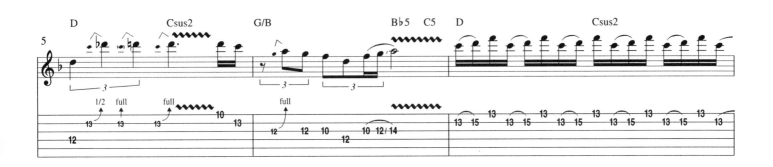

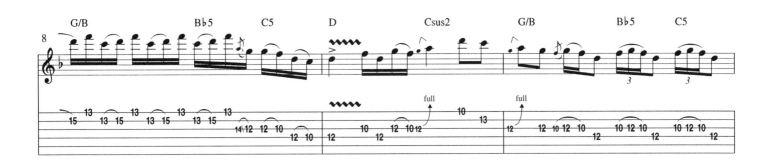

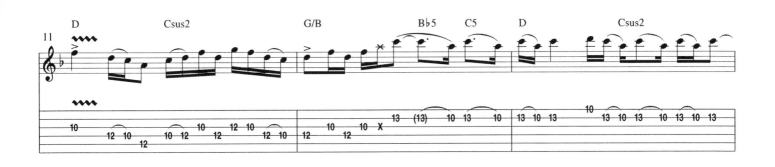

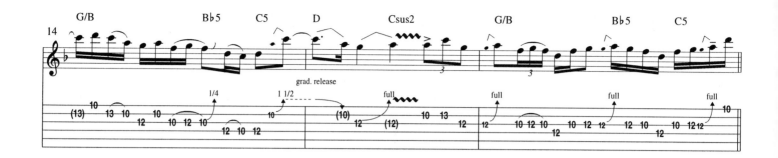

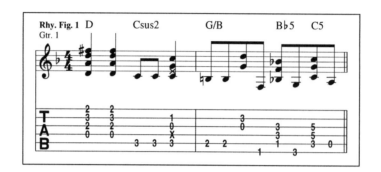

THE SUNSHINE OF YOUR LOVE
(Cream)

Words and Music by Jack Bruce, Pete Brown, and Eric Clapton

Example 1 – Introduction

Example 1 is the classic introduction to one of Cream's biggest hits, "The Sunshine of Your Love."

While the first four bars of the intro should be fairly easy to play, be sure to use left-hand muting (see Lesson 2 for "Layla") to silence the notes at the appropriate times. This should also help you stay "locked-in" tight with the bass part, which doubles the guitar melody an octave lower.

When performing the three-note chords found in measures 5 and 7, arc your index finger (which frets all chord notes played on the 6th string) slightly so that it makes contact with the other strings. This will allow you to strum the chords freely without sounding any unwanted open strings. In addition, employing a left-hand mute after each strum will help you to reproduce Clapton's staccato (short and choppy) rhythms.

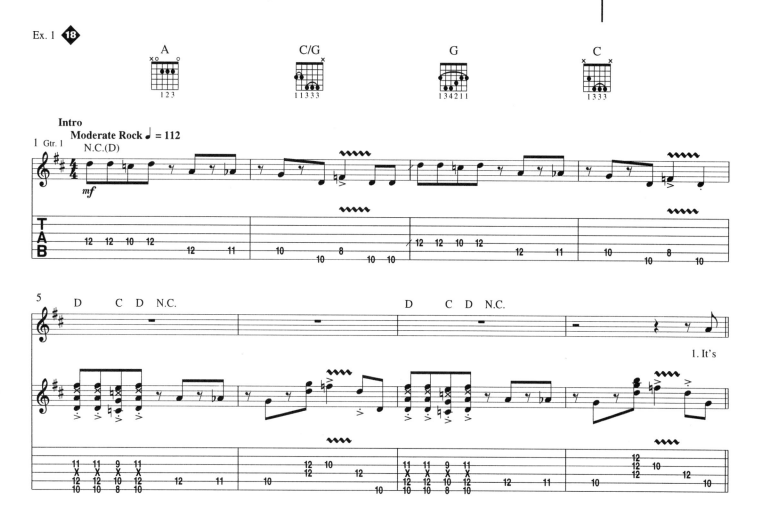

Copyright © 1968, 1973 by Dratleaf Ltd.
All Rights Administered by Unichappell Music Inc.
International Copyright Secured   All Rights Reserved

Example 2 – Verse

Throughout the verses to "The Sunshine of Your Love," Eric Clapton occasionally employs *doublestops* in order to give certain melody notes in his riff a slightly raunchier sound. For those of you unfamiliar with this technique, a doublestop is a two-note partial chord form frequently employed by both rhythm and lead guitarists to add "grit" to a riff or lick. The doublestops in this example (found in the 2nd beat of bars 2, 4, 6, and 8) can be played by simply barring your ring finger across the middle strings.

Example 3 – Chorus

As with the notes in the introduction, one of the keys to accurately performing the chorus to "The Sunshine of Your Love" involves silencing the chords at the appropriate times. While a left-hand mute would be sufficient for most of the chords, silencing the open strings in the A chord on the second beat of measures 1, 3, and 5 will require the additional use of a *right-hand palm mute.* The Xs on beats 2 and 4 of measures 2 and 4 reveal some aggressive usage of this technique, as Clapton's right hand palm (and maybe even a little bit of his pick) audibly slams down onto the strings just above the treble pickup on his guitar.

Example 4 - Guitar Solo

Eric Clapton's laid-back solo in "The Sunshine of Your Love" provides the perfect opportunity to hone your string-bending skills. If, when performing any of the many whole- or half-step bends throughout Example 4, you find your notes sounding a little "sour," you may need to work on achieving proper intonation when bending the strings. To get the right pitches, make sure that your notes bend up the appropriate distance as indicated by either the term "full" or "1/2" above the tablature. For review, a whole step (full) is equivalent to two frets, while a half step is equal to just one fret. If you're having trouble hearing the "target" pitches, play them as regular fretted notes first. For example, when you go to bend the first note of the solo, G (12th fret, 3rd string), up a whole step, first pick the A note located two frets up the neck. This is the target note that you want to remember when bending the note G up a whole step. (Note: If you can hear the target pitch, but you're just having trouble controlling the bend, reinforce the bend with your index and middle fingers. This will provide more strength with which to push the strings.)

Before attempting to learn this solo, first work on achieving proper intonation in your bends. (More advanced guitarists should practice adding vibrato to their bent notes as well.) While you can use this "target pitch" method to practice other bends, such as the *1-1/2- or 2-note* (note, not fret!) bends found in bar 8, beginning guitarists should mainly concentrate on the whole- and half-step bends. As can be observed in Example 4, these are generally used more often than any other bending technique. With frequent practice, you should eventually be able to perform clean, precise whole- or half-step bends without hesitation.

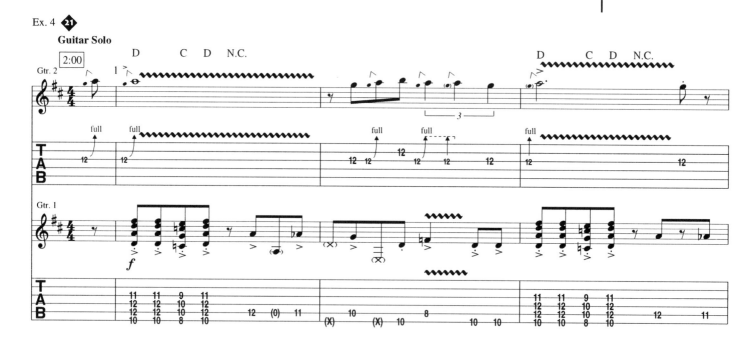

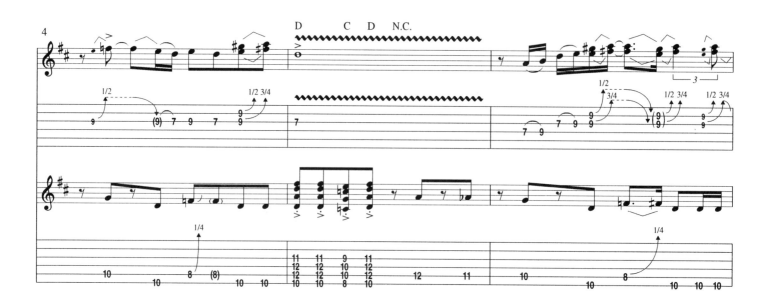

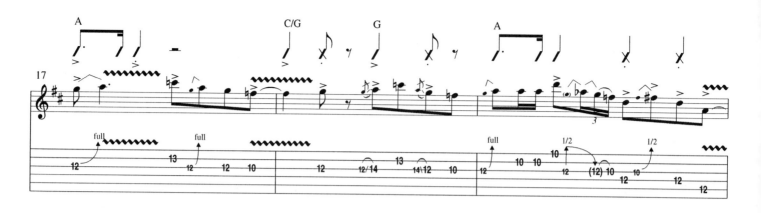

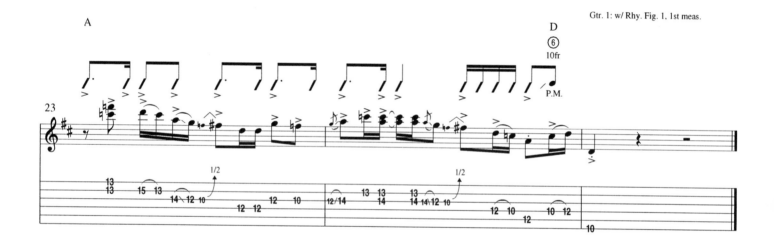

BADGE
(Cream)

Words and Music by Eric Clapton and George Harrison

Example 1 - Introduction

    By alternating heavy left-hand muted strums with chords played lightly on the upbeat, Gtr. 1 creates an interesting and unique sounding introduction to the song "Badge."

    To accurately reproduce the sound of the guitar on the original recording, be sure to observe notes marked with *sforzando* accents. Appearing as a wedge beneath certain chords in Example 1, these articulation markings indicate the use of a heavier pick attack than normally found on the other notes. When playing through the example, emphasize the stronger pick attacks on the left-hand muted strings (represented by Xs; see Lesson 2 for "Layla") while employing a more delicate strum on the rest of the chords. If you experience a bit of trouble coordinating the left-hand muting action with the right hand's alternating dynamics, slow the tempo down to a snail's pace and work through the example beat-by-beat.

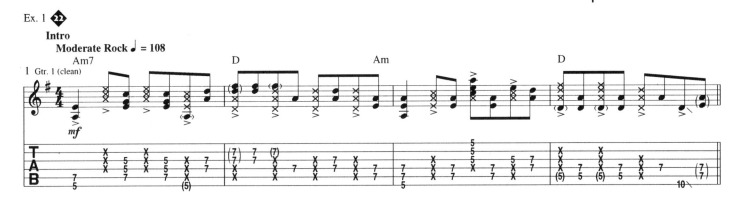

Copyright © 1969 by E.C. Music Ltd. and Apple Publishing Ltd.
All Rights on behalf of E. C. Music Ltd. for the U.S. Administered by Unichappell Music Inc.
International Copyright Secured   All Rights Reserved

Example 2 – Verse

    Playing through the verse section to "Badge" essentially involves employing the same performance techniques encountered in Example 1 (although this excerpt should be a little easier to play, as there's not so much string muting going on!). Check out the *staccato* markings found beneath the chords in the first three beats of measure 2. These small dots indicate that each chord's rhythmic duration should be slightly shorter than normal. In this case, each chord's value can be appropriately edited through the use of a simple left-hand muting action.

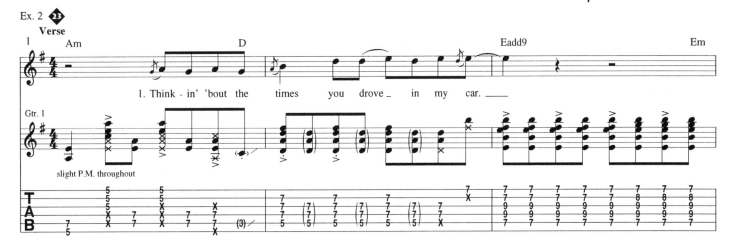

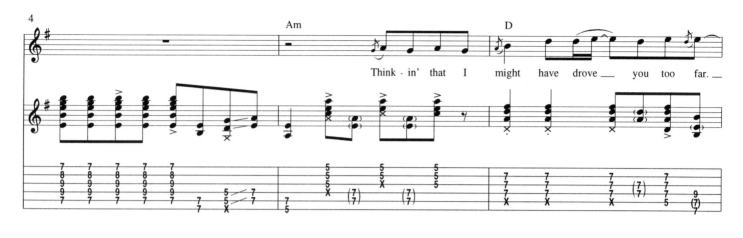

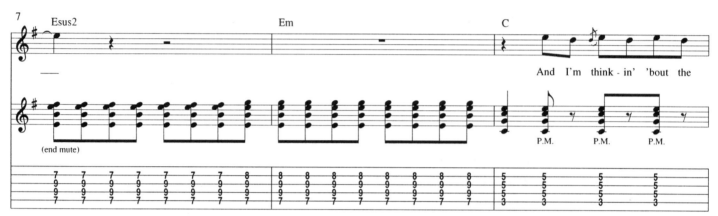

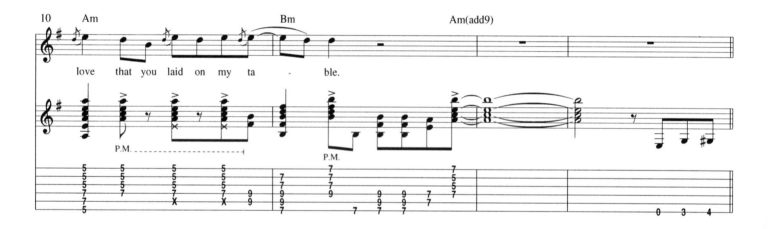

Example 3 – Bridge

For the bridge in "Badge," Eric Clapton takes a fairly common-sounding chord progression and spices it up by *arpeggiating* each chord. (The word arpeggio, originally a classical European musical term, is often used to describe when a chord's notes are broken up and played one at a time.) As we can hear, this creates a more flowing and "open" feel to the chorus, which provides a nice release from the choppier-sounding verse sections. Additionally, Eric creates a large part of this section's ambiance by allowing each of his chord's notes to ring together as long as possible. This is indicated at the beginning of the transcription excerpt by the term "let ring throughout." (Hint, hint!)

Example 4 – Guitar Solo

Throughout much of the solo in "Badge," Eric Clapton creates his more dramatic-sounding lead melodies by employing the use of a challenging bending technique known as the *prebend* and release. (In the tablature, the prebend is notated by an arrow that rises straight up from a note and points at the indicated distance of the bend.)

Prebend notes are unique from other bends in that they require you to bend a note the desired distance before it is picked. Consequently, you must depend solely on your finger's *experience* in bending notes to the appropriate distances in order to perform such a bend without actually hearing the note beforehand. To practice a prebend such as the one performed on the C note (13th fret, 2nd string) at the start of the solo, begin by first picking the note and then bending it up a whole step (as indicated by the term "full" in the transcription). Then, try and bend the same note up a whole step without the pick attack. After pre-bending, pick the note and compare it to the pitch of the previous "normal" whole step bend, making any corrections while holding the note. This comparison process will help teach your left hand exactly how much

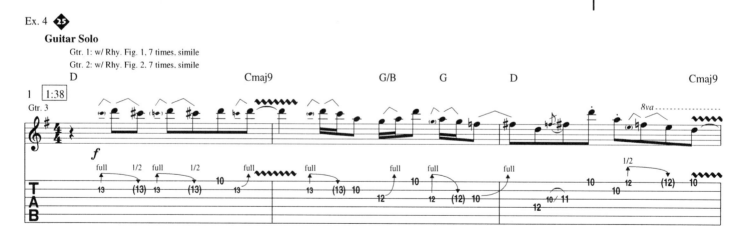

pressure to apply in order to silently bend the string up one whole step. (Obviously, you can use this pitch comparison test to similarly practice 1/2-step prebends as well.)

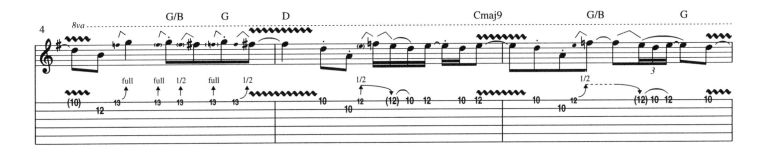
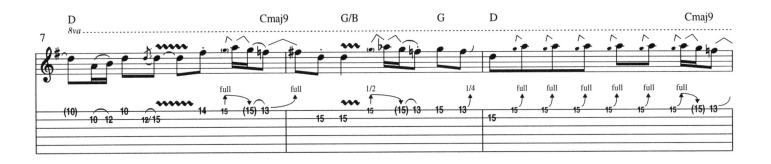
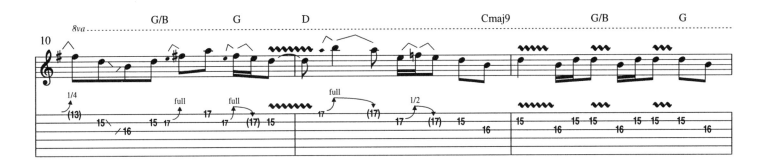
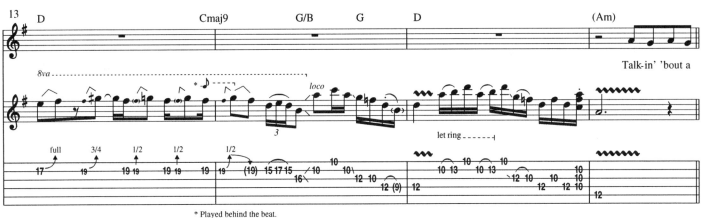

*Played behind the beat.

COVER TUNES

Throughout the history of music, musicians of past and present have always developed their playing and writing skills not only through constant practice and self-exploration, but by studying the work of their predecessors as well. (See? You're reading this book, aren't you?) Eric Clapton was no exception to this tradition. In the style of the early jazz and blues masters, Clapton "cut his teeth" on classic blues standards, using their forms and melodies to hone his own unique style of playing. Even today Clapton often pays tribute on his albums to the artists who have always interested him—the Band, Bob Dylan, Bob Marley, John J. Cale, and Don Williams, to name a few. However, because Eric artistically performs these covers in his own style and voice, few people realize that many of Clapton's biggest hits are actually revamped versions of music previously recorded by other artists. For example, "Cocaine" and "After Midnight" were originally recorded by John J. Cale, while Cream's smash hit, "Crossroads," was actually written by legendary blues great, Robert Johnson.

The following are some excerpts from three tunes that Clapton borrowed from other artists.

Example 1 – I Shot the Sheriff (chorus)

Words and Music by Bob Marley

To play through this reggae classic by Bob Marley, try using the pendulum strumming method discussed in the verse lesson for "Layla."

Copyright © 1974 PolyGram International Publishing, Inc.
International Copyright Secured   All Rights Reserved

Example 2 – Knockin' on Heaven's Door (chorus)

Music and Lyrics by Bob Dylan

Again, revealing his influence from Marley, Clapton takes this Bob Dylan hit and turns it into his own rasta-fest! Notice how Eric contrasts the muted, definitive reggae-style chords played on the upbeats (Gtr. 2, shown in slash notation) with lofty, sustained chords colored by a wah-wah pedal (Gtr. 1). Jam on, mon!

Ex. 2

Copyright © 1973, 1976 by Special Rider Music
International Copyright Secured   All Rights Reserved   Used by Permission

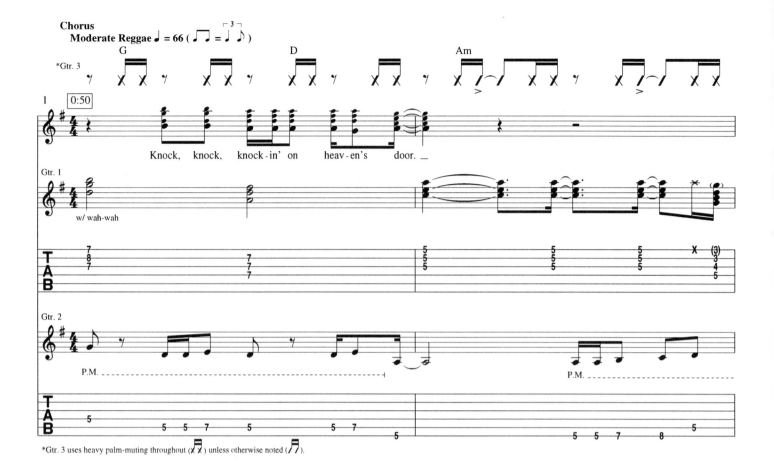

Example 3 – Little Wing

This classic by the late Jimi Hendrix has been heavily covered by artists throughout the last few years (pop icon Sting and rockers Skid Row to name a few), and now we can check out the version Eric Clapton recorded with Derek and the Dominoes back in 1970.

43

The chord progression in the example for "Little Wing" repeatedly plays throughout the entire song, making the tune a potential catalyst for an awesome jam session. (There aren't many lyrics to remember either!) A powerfully moving song, "Little Wing" should be included in every guitarist's repertoire!

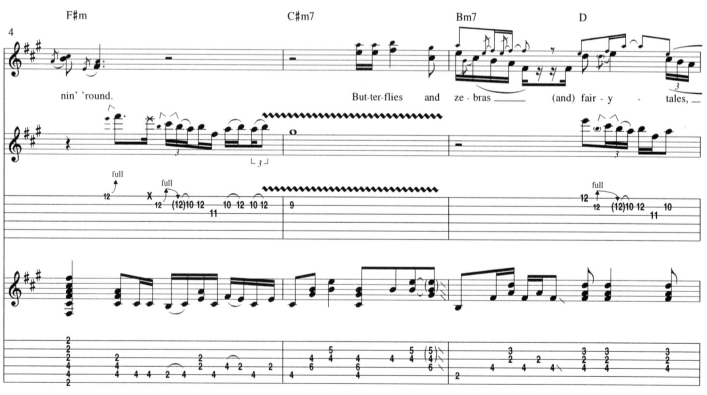

Copyright © 1968 by EXPERIENCE HENDRIX, L.L.C.
All Rights Controlled and Administered by Don Williams Music Group Inc.
All Rights Reserved   International Copyright Secured

CROSSROADS
(CROSS ROAD BLUES)
(Cream)
Words and Music by Robert Johnson

Example 1 - Introduction

In "Crossroads," Eric Clapton provides us with a great example of some totally off-the-wall soloing over a standard 12-bar blues chord progression.

Example 1 depicts the first 12 measures of the song, where Eric plays through the tune's "head," or main melodic theme. When playing through the introduction, use an index finger barre across the 2nd–4th strings. This will allow you to easily play the double stops throughout the excerpt without hesitation. Also, be careful not to overdo the 1/4- and 1/2-step bends performed on the C note (3rd fret, 5th string) at the end of each measure in the first eight bars. While he occasionally bends this note up a 1/2 step, for the most part, Eric uses 1/4-step bends to produce a bluesy, dirtier-sounding quality to his riff.

For those of you unfamiliar with this subtle bending technique, the *1/4 step bend* involves bending a note up the distance equal to half a fret. Because there is no fretted equivalent to this pitch, you'll need to use your ears to listen for the appropriate halfway point between the two frets. When performing the 1/4-step bends found in Example 1, *pull* the string away from yourself (or towards the higher strings) rather than pushing it upwards. This will help minimize your chances of overshooting the bend.

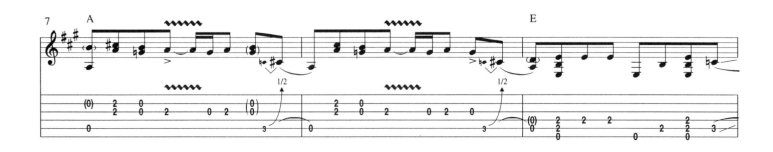

Copyright © (1978) 1991 King Of Spades Music
All Rights Reserved   Used by Permission

Example 2 – Verse

In the verse sections to "Crossroads," you'll notice that Eric Clapton breaks up his main riff (the 12-bar head we studied in Example 1) so that every two bars are replaced with a standard, bluesy rhythm guitar figure (see bars 1-2). Following a similar approach to his accompaniment of Duane Allman's solo in "Have You Ever Loved a Woman," Eric is laying back and simplifying his guitar part while singing in order to keep the instrumentation from getting too busy and stealing attention from the vocals.

During the vocal parts, Eric keeps his guitar playing under control through the use of a technique known as *palm muting* (indicated by the abbreviation P.M.). Used to create strong, pumping rhythms, palm muting is a maneuver that involves lightly resting the fleshy side of your palm on the strings near the bridge as you pick. As this palm pressure reduces string vibration, the sound and duration of the notes involved are directly affected by the amount of right-hand pressure you apply to the string. Increasing the pressure generally results in quieter notes with shorter rhythmic durations. When performing Example 2, you'll need to apply a fairly heavy-handed palm mute in order to best re-create the sounds heard on the original recording.

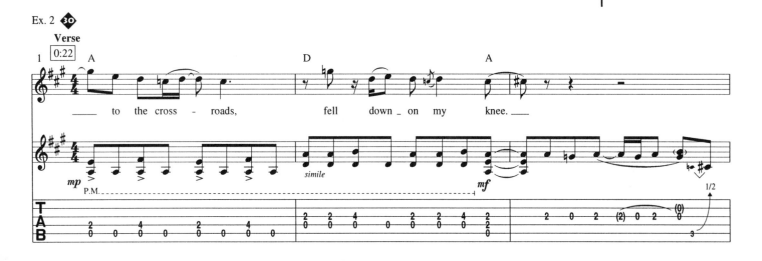

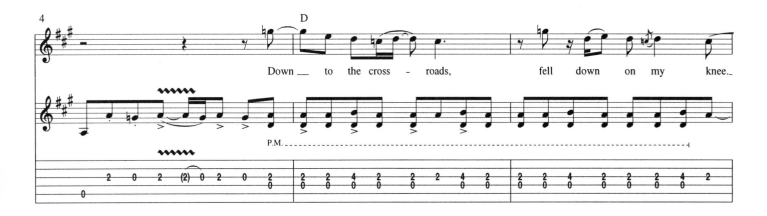

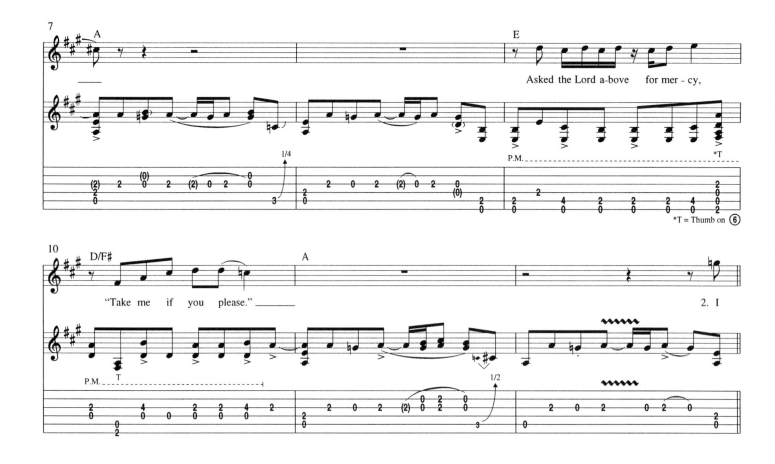

Example 3 – 1st Guitar Solo

Hailed by many as one of his greatest solos to date, Clapton's lead in "Crossroads" provides an awesome example of some balls-to-the-wall wailing over a 12-bar blues progression.

Eric creates some interesting mood changes throughout his solo by constantly switching between the pentatonic major and the pentatonic minor scales. If you're not that familiar with the pentatonic major scale, check out the chord charts provided in the "Pentatonic Scale Positions" lesson. Notes in parentheses depict the root or starting positions for each major pentatonic scale. By referring to these scale charts, you should see that the major pentatonic licks found in measures 1-2 fall into pattern 1 (located at the 2nd fret), while at the end of bar 2, the major pentatonic licks slide up a couple frets to the next pentatonic position, pattern 2. Clapton then switches to the pentatonic *minor* sound in bar 4 by jamming out some licks in pattern 1, now located at the 5th fret. While the remaining licks, for the most part, stay in this pentatonic pattern, Eric often hints at the major tonality by working the note C♯ (6th fret, 3rd string) into his licks. (C♯ belongs to the key of A major.)

Note: Another popular way to remember the major pentatonic shapes is to take the minor pentatonic box shapes for a particular key and simply slide them down three frets. However, if you choose to use this method, be sure to practice the scales from their roots. Otherwise, you'll just end up playing a minor pentatonic scale in a different key.

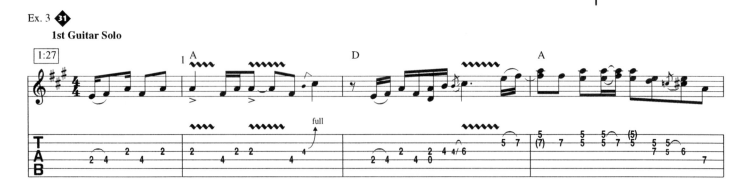

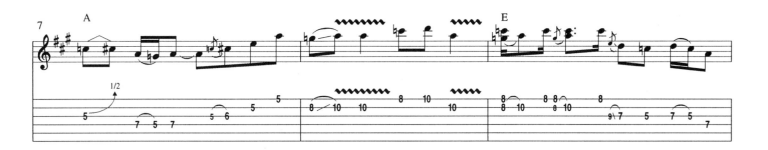

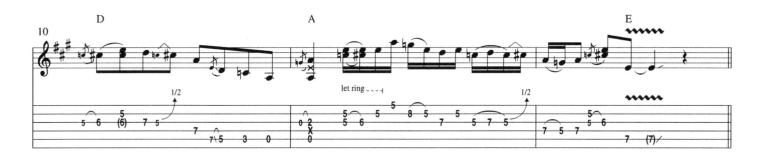

Example 4 – 2nd Guitar Solo

In this second guitar solo, Clapton significantly increases the song's energy level by launching into a volley of blistering licks high up on the fretboard of his guitar. Although the licks may sound a bit intimidating at first, a quick study of the transcription will reveal that most of the licks fall easily into pattern 1, located one octave (12 frets) higher than previously positioned.

By learning Eric Clapton's solos in "Crossroads," you'll receive a good head start in playing lead guitar over a 12-bar blues progression. Even if you don't intend to learn these particular excerpts note-for-note, go through the transcriptions anyway and see what notes Eric does or doesn't emphasize over certain chords in the progression. Doing so will not only give you some insight into Clapton's personal style of playing, but will also teach you a little bit about playing *melodically* over chord changes.

Ex. 4

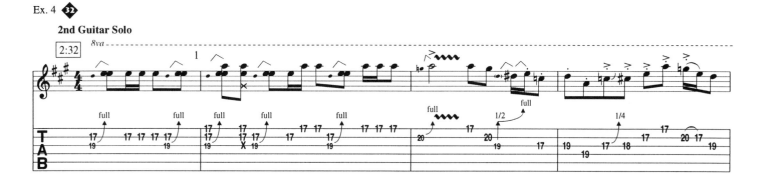

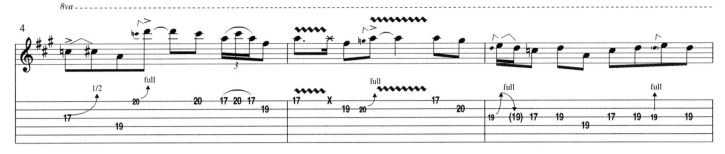
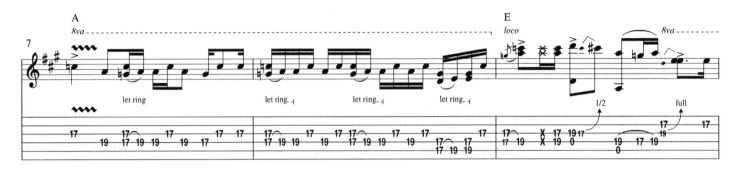
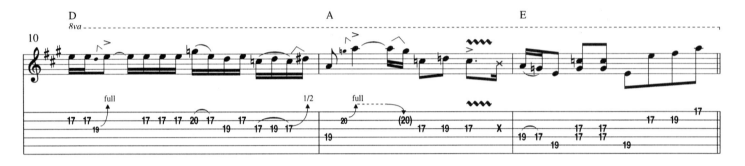

COCAINE
Words and Music by John J. Cale

Example 1 – Introduction

As in "Layla," Clapton overdubs several guitar parts in his introduction to "Cocaine" to create a thicker, more lively-sounding guitar track. Those of you who may want to perform this tune in a small band situation should primarily concentrate on learning the first guitar part (Gtr. 1) shown in *slash notation* above the top staff system. (This is the featured guitar part on the *Signature Licks* recording.) While the other guitar parts are obviously an integral part of the song on the original recording, neither guitar 2 nor 3 could effectively present the overall feel of Clapton's riff on their own. Instead, save these additional lead guitar overdubs for a two- or three-guitar arrangement.

When working with slash notation, remember to consult the chord charts provided at the beginning of the song in order to ensure you'll be playing the correct version of each chord. Also, if you're not that used to reading basic rhythms, such as the ones used in the slash notation for "Cocaine," you'll need to refer to the recording often. If you don't know how to read basic rhythms at all, I would suggest picking up a beginning level guitar method book at your local music store, as many transcription books and magazines now utilize this slash notation method! Whether you're a beginning guitarist or not, learning how to read and write music notation will not only enable you to teach yourself virtually any style of music, but will allow you to preserve those spontaneous song ideas on paper when you don't have immediate access to a tape machine!

Example 2 – Guitar Solo

Copyright © 1975 AUDIGRAM MUSIC
A Division of AUDIGRAM, INC., P.O. Box 635, Nashville, TN 37202
All Rights Reserved   International Copyright Secured

Eric Clapton's solo in "Cocaine" makes for a great study in *unison bends.* A unison bend involves bending a note up to the same pitch of another note on the next highest string (usually a whole step higher). To play a unison bend such as the one at the end of measure 4, pick both notes at the same time and let them ring together when performing the bend. Use the top note as your "target pitch" for the whole-step bend from A (14th fret, 3rd string) to B. (Once again, if you have trouble controlling the pitch of the bend, add your middle and ring fingers for extra "muscle.") Once you've mastered the unison bends throughout bars 4–6, move on to the ones in bars 18 and 19. Throughout these measures, we find a common variation on the technique where Clapton picks the top note of the unison bend (E, 12th fret, 1st string) *before* attacking the lower note (D, 15th fret, 2nd string). When played up to speed, it almost sounds like the bent note (D) is trying to chase or catch up to the pitch of the target note (E).

Ex. 2
Guitar Solo

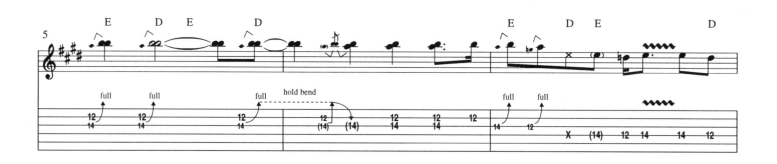
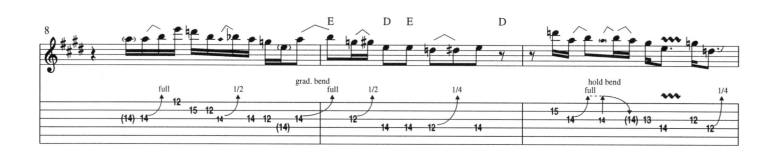
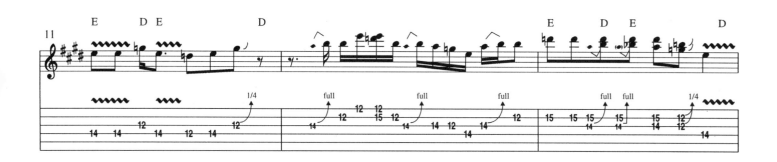
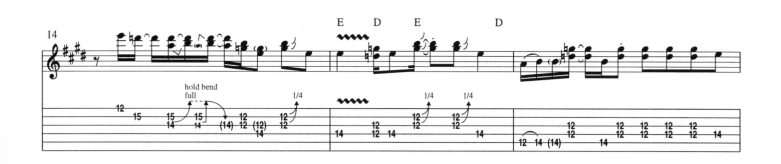

53

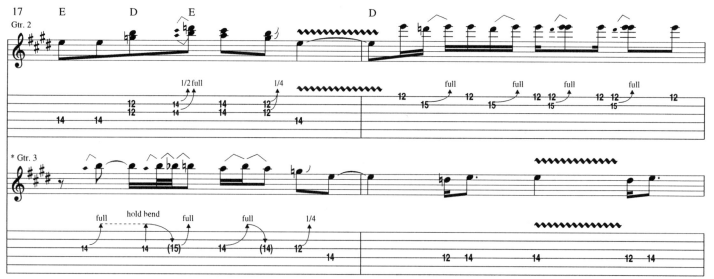
* Not audible on *Signature Licks* recording.

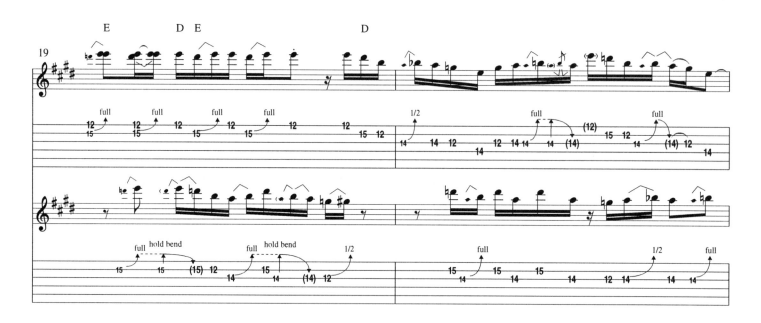

* Played ahead of the beat.

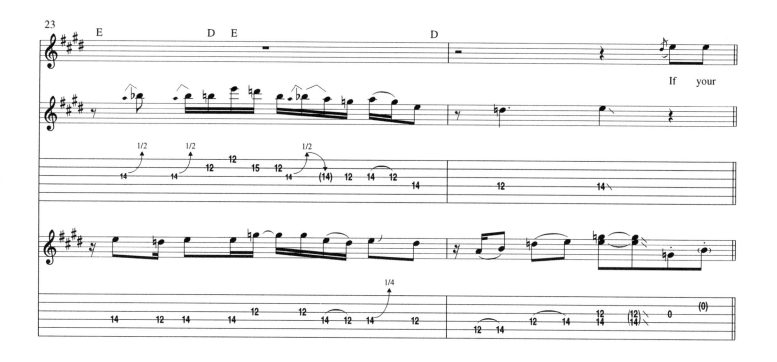

WONDERFUL TONIGHT

Words and Music by Eric Clapton

Example 1 – Introduction

On the *Signature Licks* recording, Gtr. 1 is the featured guitar part, as it presents the main chord progression for the tune in its entirety. However, the other guitar overdubs are included in the left speaker channel should you want to study and/or teach them to another guitarist for use in a live performance.

When performing the main guitar part to "Wonderful Tonight," you'll need to work out a right hand picking pattern using either *alternate* or *economy* picking techniques. Although you could use all down-pick attacks to play through the arpeggiated chords in Example 1, your rhythms will probably sound a bit choppier than if you employed the alternate picking technique. Alternate picking, as the name suggests, involves strictly alternating the direction of your pick attack (down up, down up, etc...) for *every* note. The technique eliminates a lot of unnecessary right-hand movement in your picking, which in turn, allows your arm to relax and produce smoother, cleaner rhythms. However, while alternate picking offers "crisper," more precise rhythms, the method does require a great deal of practice and patience to perfect. If you have trouble getting used to alternate picking, perhaps the economy picking method will better suit your playing style. (While economy picking will work fine in most cases, it is not as clean as alternate picking when used on high speed passages.)

With economy picking, you still alternately pick notes, *except* when moving from one string to another. When moving to a higher string, use consecutive downstrokes, letting the pick "fall" onto the next string. Likewise, when moving to a lower string, use two consecutive upstrokes. Picking this way helps reduce muscular stress on the tendons in your right hand and forearm, making certain licks easier to manage. This method should also help you perform some of the more difficult string skips found throughout the song. To help get you started, I've provided a few bars of economy picking prompts below the tablature system for the main guitar part.

By working on a specific picking pattern for the chords in "Wonderful Tonight," you should be able to easily play through the tune without hesitating on certain chords or accidentally picking any wrong notes. However, regardless of which picking technique you choose to employ, try becoming familiar with both, as you may find that different musical situations will prefer one method over the other!

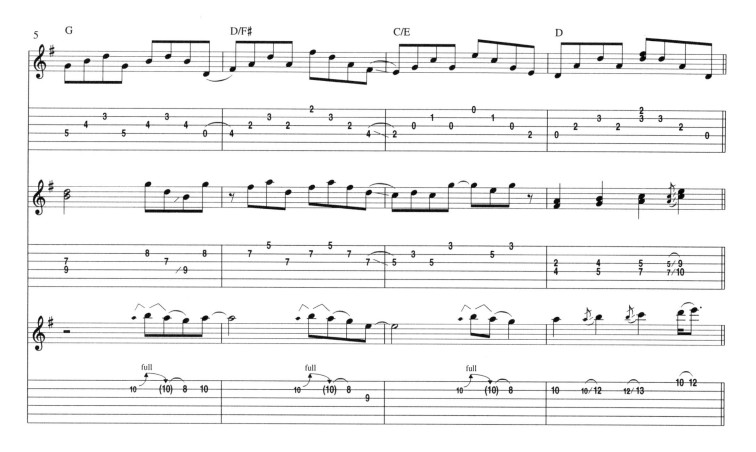

Copyright © 1977 by Eric Patrick Clapton
All Rights for the U.S. Administered by Unichappell Music Inc.
International Copyright Secured   All Rights Reserved

Example 2 – Verse, Chorus, Bridge, Interlude

Too often, beginning guitarists will devote a considerable amount of energy learning a song's main riff or solo licks while hardly spending any time working on the tune as a whole piece of music. Consequently, the student never actually develops the sense of timing and physical endurance required to play through an entire song. Jam sessions with other musicians turn into a game of "name that tune," as the student's entire repertoire virtually consists of a bunch of short riffs and solo snippets. In Example 2 for "Wonderful Tonight," I've provided a great exercise in endurance playing, as the excerpt is over two minutes long.

You'll first need to work on mastering the music before trying to play along with the recording. Beginning players should memorize the entire guitar part so that they can concentrate their attention on the guitar rather than on the sheet music. More experienced players, however, can probably get away with just following along with the transcription after a few minutes of focused study. If you haven't learned many songs from start to finish, practice this example repeatedly until you can perform the entire excerpt without your hands "poopin' out" on you. This repetitive practice will help you begin to develop the physical endurance you'll need to comfortably perform songs over several minutes in length. In addition, you can help ensure accurate timing (rhythms) throughout the example by trying to keep the muscles in your forearms and hands *relaxed,* as excess tension or fatigue in these areas usually results in a rhythmically sloppy performance.

Hopefully, by working through this entire example for "Wonderful Tonight," you'll realize that there are many more factors involved in learning a song than just mastering the main lick or riff.

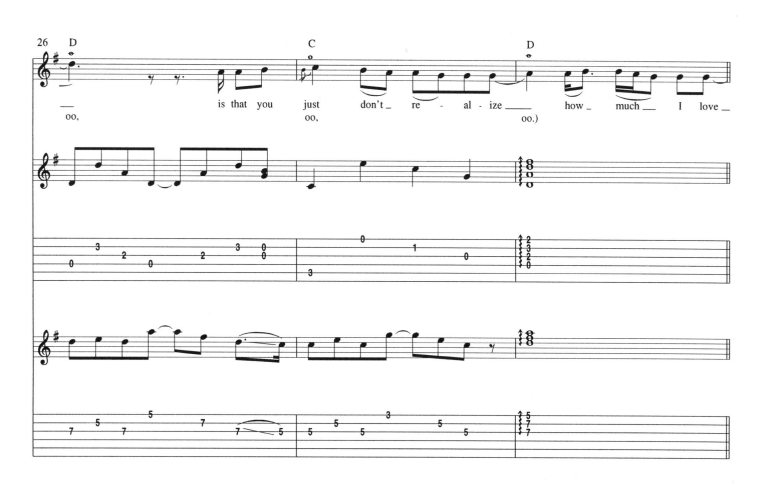

LAY DOWN SALLY

Words and Music by Eric Clapton, Marcy Levy and George Terry

Example 1 – Introduction

To get through this fast-paced riff for "Lay Down Sally," similarly follow the practice guidelines I suggested you use on the solo licks in Example 4 for "Have You Ever Loved a Woman."

1. First, roughly go through the transcription to get a general feel for the riff.

2. Listen to the recording often! However, don't play the entire song each time, just listen to the few measures that you're working on.

3. If you find the length or complexity of the example intimidating, break it up into smaller, more manageable pieces. If you have to, just work on one or two measures at a time.

4. When performing the example, start out slowly. This way, you'll be able to hear better and correct any trouble spots in your playing.

Copyright © 1977 by Eric Patrick Clapton and Throat Music Ltd.
All Rights for the U.S. Administered by Unichappell Music Inc.
International Copyright Secured   All Rights Reserved

*Played ahead of the beat.

Example 2 – Verse and Chorus

Example 2 provides another opportunity for you to work on your performance endurance (see Lesson 2 for "Wonderful Tonight"), as this excerpt is over a full minute in length.

When playing through the example, listen to the recording carefully to hear *how much* palm-muting technique should be applied to re-create each of the guitar parts. As indicated in the transcription, Clapton uses a very light right-hand touch on the main guitar in order to keep the part sounding mellow throughout the verse sections. On the slightly louder part played by Guitar 2, he employs a heavier mute to produce shorter, choppier rhythms. The different amount of palm pressure between the two parts serves to create some additional rhythmic contrast which helps to separate the two guitars in the overall mix.

Example 3 – Guitar Solo

Once you've gone through and worked with Eric Clapton's licks in Example 3 for "Lay Down Sally," pan your stereo's balance control over to the left channel and try coming up with your own solo. Be sure to use Eric's licks as a springboard for your own ideas, rather than copying them note-for-note. Here's a good exercise to help you do this: First, analyze Eric's solo, looking for some common traits that are shared among his licks and solo melodies. Then, use the similarities you've discovered as guidelines, or boundaries, to follow when coming up with a solo of your own. For example, the two more obvious traits I found consistent throughout the solo are:

1. Clapton performs most of his licks in the 5th position A minor pentatonic scale, and

2. Throughout virtually the entire solo, he employs only 8th and 1/4-note rhythms in his licks!

Using these commonalities as parameters for soloing over the backing track, you would then confine your licks within the 5th position minor pentatonic pattern #1 scale, and employ basic, straight-ahead rhythms involving notes of only an eighth or quarter note in length. This type of creative practicing forces you to think a little more about your choice of notes, and will hopefully shed some new light onto your present playing habits.

69

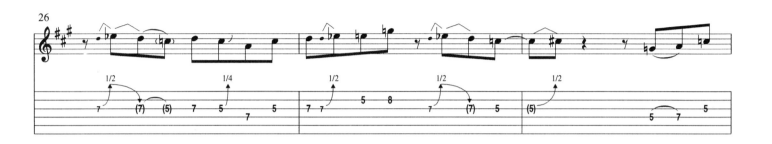

71

AFTER MIDNIGHT
Words and Music by John J. Cale

Example 1 – Verse

Performing the lightning-fast rhythm guitar part in "After Midnight" will require some tricky right- and left-hand coordination. To help get you started, I've provided a suggested right-hand strumming pattern in prompts between the staff and tablature for the first couple of measures. (You may notice that this pattern closely follows the pendulum strumming method discussed in lesson 2 for "Layla.") For the left hand's part, you'll need to use an index finger barre across the 2nd–4th strings to fret the C and E♭ chords (located throughout Example 1 at the 5th and 8th frets, respectively), while using a ring finger barre to perform the F chord at the 10th fret. Note that a quick left-hand mute after each chord attack is required in order to best re-create the spunky rhythms heard on the original recording.

© 1966 WARNER-TAMERLANE PUBLISHING CORP. (Renewed)
All Rights Reserved

Example 2 – Guitar Solo

In the first eight bars of his solo for "After Midnight," Eric Clapton repeats a simple four-bar melody in order to create a memorable, melodic-sounding interlude. By repeating his solo motif like this, Clapton allows the listener (especially the non-musicians) another chance to absorb the beautiful, vocal-like melodies in his licks. In bars 11-12, we can see where he uses repetition on a slightly smaller scale, composing a rapid-fire lick by repeating a descending three-note melody over and over.

By employing such repetition techniques similarly in your own solos, you'll be able to effectively present a cool-sounding melodic idea to an audience that may otherwise hear it as just another fast flurry of notes!

ACOUSTIC RIFFS

While much of Clapton's best music was originally written on the electric guitar, in more recent years Eric has devoted a good deal of attention towards composing music on the acoustic guitar. In 1992 Eric was invited to perform a set of all-acoustic material on the MTV television network. The performance included his then recent acoustic hit, "Tears in Heaven," as well as some traditional blues tunes such as "Malted Milk," by Robert Johnson, and "Alberta." The MTV show went over so well that the performance was later released as an album entitled *Eric Clapton/Unplugged*.

Below are excerpts from two previous Clapton hits, "Layla" and "Before You Accuse Me (Take A Look At Yourself)," which Eric revamped for his MTV acoustic performance. The new arrangement for "Layla" was received so well that it was eventually released as a single to help promote the new album.

Example 1 – Layla (Chorus)

Compared to the original version shown at the beginning of the book, this acoustic arrangement of the 1970s Derek and the Dominoes hit sounds almost like an entirely different song!

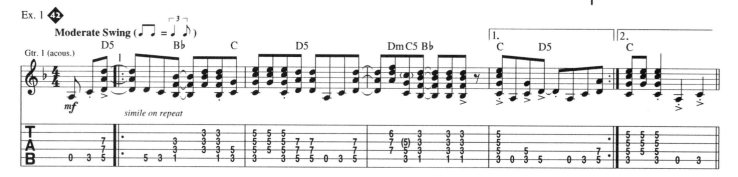

Copyright © 1970 by Eric Patrick Clapton and Throat Music Ltd.
All Rights for the U.S. Administered by Unichappell Music Inc.
International Copyright Secured   All Rights Reserved

Example 2 – Before You Accuse Me (Take A Look At Yourself) (Verse)

Words and Music by Eugene McDaniels

A considerably mellower version than the one on the *Journeyman* album, the "MTV" acoustic arrangement for "Before You Accuse Me (Take A Look At Yourself)" provides a great example of delta-blues guitar played Eric Clapton style. Just for kicks, try performing this excerpt first with, and then without, a guitar pick. You'll probably find that strumming with your fingers produces a "rounder," more traditional sound, while also allowing you to effortlessly perform the string skipping found in measures 8 and 9.

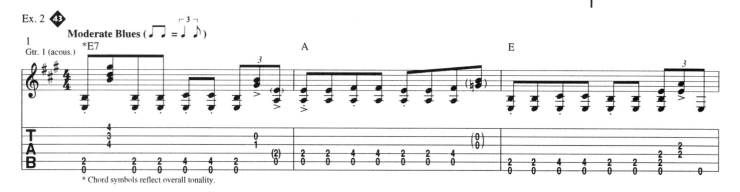

* Chord symbols reflect overall tonality.

© Copyright 1957 (Renewed 1985) WINDSWEPT PACIFIC ENTERTAINMENT CO. d/b/a LONGITUDE MUSIC CO.
All Rights Reserved

TEARS IN HEAVEN
Words and Music by Eric Clapton and Will Jennings

Example 1 – Introduction and Verse

As indicated in the transcription, Eric Clapton performs "Tears in Heaven" finger style on a nylon-string (classical) acoustic guitar. While you obviously don't need to own a classical guitar to play "Tears in Heaven," you will need to check out the *right-hand fingerpicking* in advance. I've provided some right-hand fingering suggestions (employing classical-style labeling) below the tablature system for the main guitar part (Gtr. 1). For those of you unfamiliar with the classical, or "pima," right-hand labeling: p = index finger, i = middle finger, m = ring finger, a = pinky, t = thumb. Remember, however, that these fingering examples are merely *suggestions* and depict only one of many possibilities! Feel free to experiment and come up with your own versions.

In order to keep the backing tracks "open" for you to more easily practice along with the recording, I have omitted the second guitar part from the signature licks recording. However, as the two guitar parts are similar, I'm sure you'll have no problem learning the missing part on your own. You may even find the two guitar parts are virtually interchangeable! For example, try playing through the first four measures of Example 1, switching guitar parts every measure. In measure one you'll follow the music in the top staff system, measure two the bottom staff, measure three the top again, and so on. Experimenting like this will help you come up with your own solo arrangement for performing "Tears in Heaven" all by yourself.

Copyright © 1992 by E.C. Music Limited and Blue Sky Rider Songs
All Rights for E.C. Music Limited Administered by Unichappell Music Inc.
International Copyright Secured   All Rights Reserved

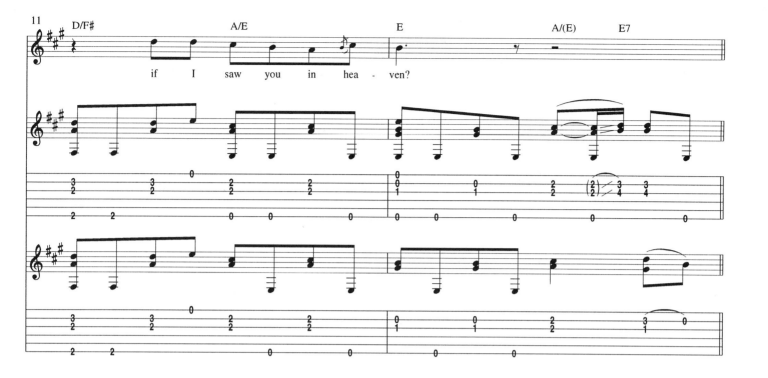

Example 2 – Chorus

While fingerpicking the chords in the first four bars of Example 2 may initially seem difficult or awkward, fretting all the notes that will be played throughout the measure ahead of time will help cut down on any confusion for the left hand. To do this, simply pay attention to what chord is actually being played in each measure. For example, while your right hand is required to jump around on different strings throughout the first measure, your left hand can sit on easy street while holding down a regular ol' F# minor barre chord at the second fret. A close examination of the chord in measure two will reveal that your best performance will be accomplished if you either barre your index finger all the way across the 1st fret, or use your thumb to fret the E# note on the 1st fret of the 6th string. When possible, try to similarly fret other chords' notes in advance in order to prevent your left hand from having to constantly change finger positions. Such foresight can only promote a smoother, more comfortable performance of the music!

Example 3 – Bridge

With a chord change occurring every two beats, playing through Example 3 will require a combination of *precise* right-hand fingerpicking and left-hand finger positioning. Use the fingerpicking method taught in the first lesson to create your own picking pattern, while referring to the chord symbols above the system to help you remember the chords for the left-hand fingerings.

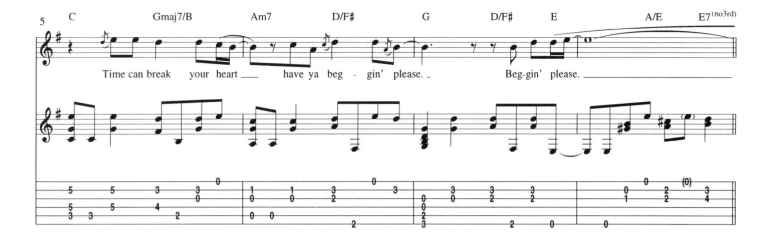

Example 4 – Interlude

While the harmonized leads in the interlude section for "Tears in Heaven" are performed by two guitars, a close look at the transcription will reveal that, with a little planning, it is possible to perform both parts on one guitar. One way to perform the harmonies found in the last four bars of the example involves using your index finger to fret the higher note in each harmony, while employing your middle finger to fret the lower harmony note. However, approaching some of the notes with the legato slides within the melodies may prove a bit awkward, if not impossible, when using this method. (Your index and middle fingers would have to squish in next to one another on the same fret!) As a result, you'll probably need to either adjust the fingering or employ an index finger barre for harmony notes that appear adjacent to each other on the same fret. At any rate, when determining what fingerings to ultimately use on the harmony parts in Example 4, don't be afraid to similarly omit a slide technique or two. Such changes in music are often necessary when arranging multiple parts for performance on a single instrument.

PRETENDING
Words and Music by Jerry Williams

Example 1 – Introduction

Keeping his leads in the introduction fairly straightforward, Eric produces a more memorable, melodic-sounding solo than if he had just cut loose on some pentatonic blues scales. To help provide a bit of tonal variety, Eric colors his guitar sound with a wah-wah pedal and a skillfully coaxed hint of feedback from his guitar amp. However, I wouldn't suggest you attempt to re-create this feedback yourself unless you have a loud amplifier, good ear plugs, and some forgiving neighbors!

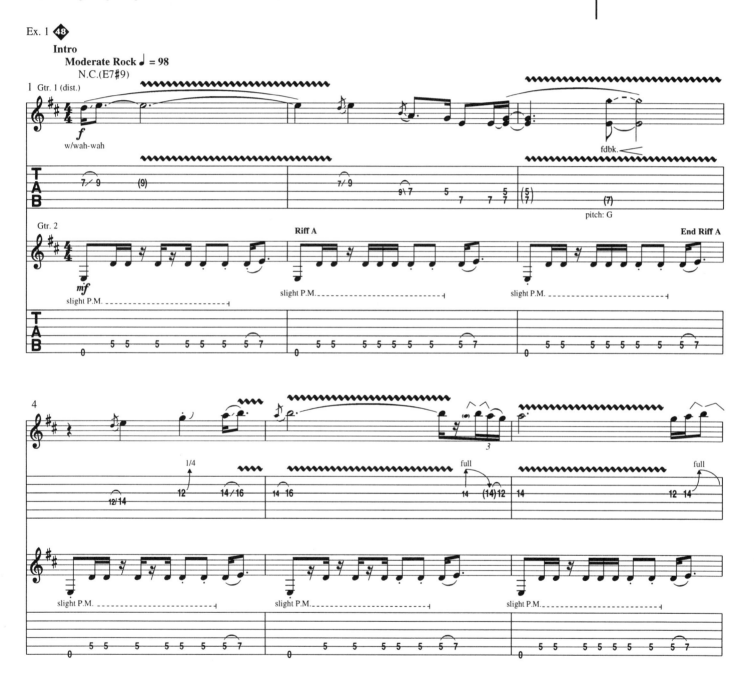

Copyright © 1985 by Careers-BMG Music Publishing, Inc., Hamstein Music and Urge Music
International Copyright Secured   All Rights Reserved

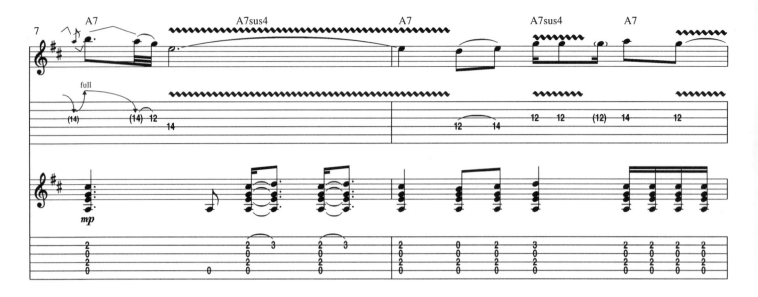

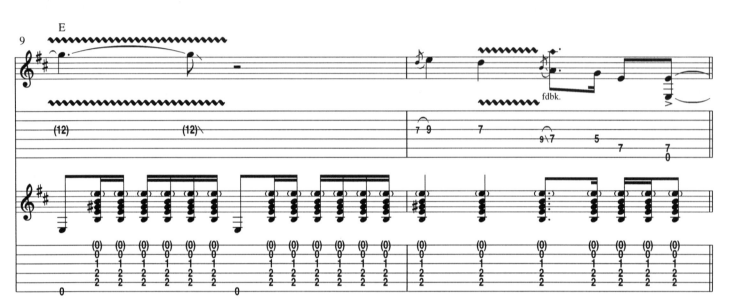

Example 2 – Chorus

Throughout the chorus to "Pretending," Eric plays some sweet-sounding leads that really add to the overall feel of the tune. While in many cases performing solo licks during a song's chorus tends to distract the listener from the vocal lyrics and melodies, in this instance Eric shows us how, when done tastefully and sparingly, a lead guitar melody can sometimes provide just the right accompaniment to make a good song sound even better.

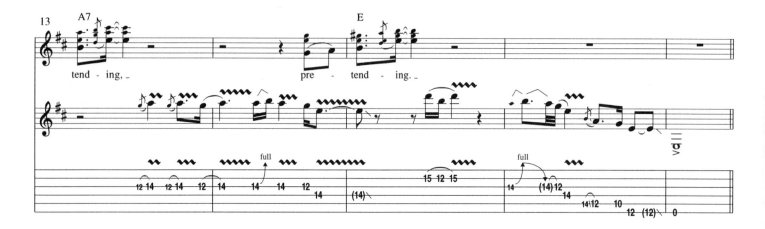

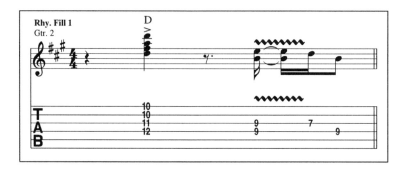

Example 3 – Guitar Solo

In his solo for "Pretending," Eric Clapton performs some wailing licks that seem to jump out of the speakers and sing to you personally! While the techniques he uses within the solo are fairly basic, the reason why Clapton's playing is so full of emotion is because he's truly connected to the guitar through his "inner ear." This is more commonly referred to as "playing from the heart," and describes a level of playing that transcends scale charts, finger positions, and memorized licks.

To approach this level of musical awareness yourself, you must come to realize that music is created from within yourself! One way to practice cultivating this talent is to create a short melody in your head and then attempt to play it on the guitar. While at first you may only be able to pull this off with simple melodies, as you progress, you'll eventually be able to perform full-blown licks composed entirely in your head (or should I say, heart)!

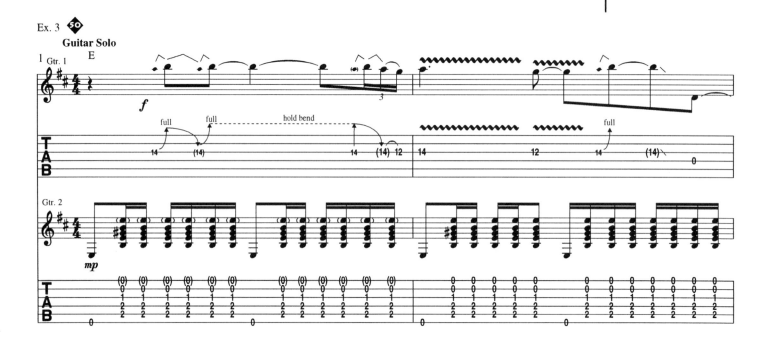

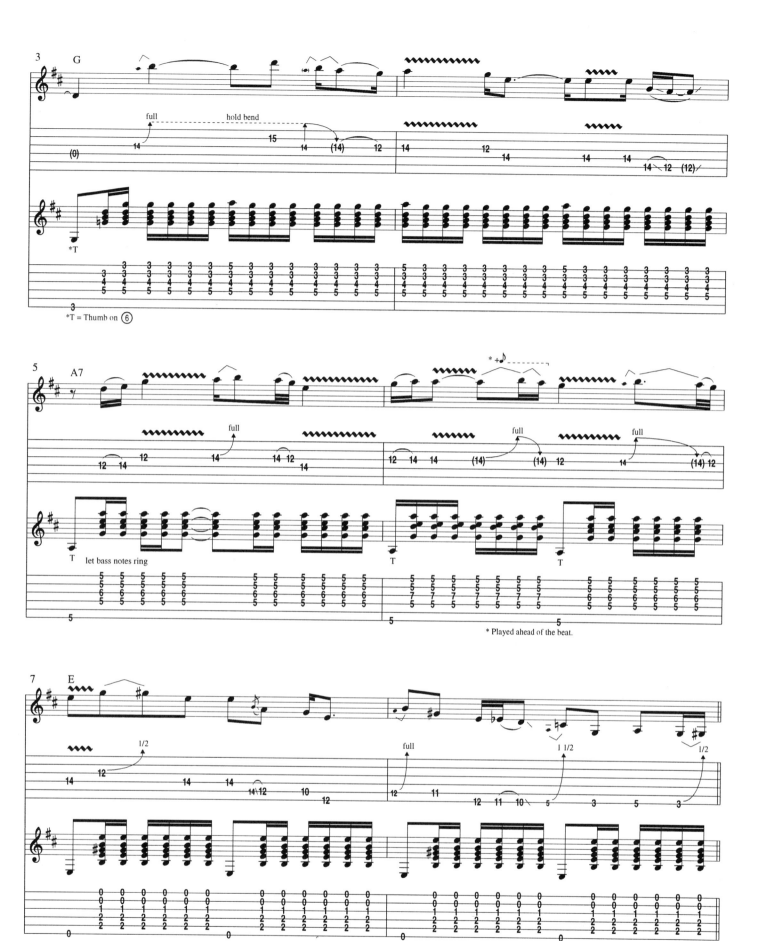

GUITAR NOTATION LEGEND

Guitar Music can be notated three different ways: on a *musical staff*, in *tablature*, and in *rhythm slashes*.

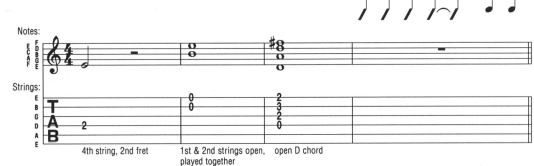

RHYTHM SLASHES are written above the staff. Strum chords in the rhythm indicated. Use the chord diagrams found at the top of the first page of the transcription for the appropriate chord voicings. Round noteheads indicate single notes.

THE MUSICAL STAFF shows pitches and rhythms and is divided by bar lines into measures. Pitches are named after the first seven letters of the alphabet.

TABLATURE graphically represents the guitar fingerboard. Each horizontal line represents a string, and each number represents a fret.

HALF-STEP BEND: Strike the note and bend up 1/2 step.

WHOLE-STEP BEND: Strike the note and bend up one step.

GRACE NOTE BEND: Strike the note and bend up as indicated. The first note does not take up any time.

SLIGHT (MICROTONE) BEND: Strike the note and bend up 1/4 step.

BEND AND RELEASE: Strike the note and bend up as indicated, then release back to the original note. Only the first note is struck.

PRE-BEND: Bend the note as indicated, then strike it.

VIBRATO: The string is vibrated by rapidly bending and releasing the note with the fretting hand.

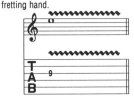

WIDE VIBRATO: The pitch is varied to a greater degree by vibrating with the fretting hand.

HAMMER-ON: Strike the first (lower) note with one finger, then sound the higher note (on the same string) with another finger by fretting it without picking.

PULL-OFF: Place both fingers on the notes to be sounded. Strike the first note and without picking, pull the finger off to sound the second (lower) note.

LEGATO SLIDE: Strike the first note and then slide the same fret-hand finger up or down to the second note. The second note is not struck.

SHIFT SLIDE: Same as legato slide, except the second note is struck.

TRILL: Very rapidly alternate between the notes indicated by continuously hammering on and pulling off.

TAPPING: Hammer ("tap") the fret indicated with the pick-hand index or middle finger and pull off to the note fretted by the fret hand.

NATURAL HARMONIC: Strike the note while the fret-hand lightly touches the string directly over the fret indicated.

PINCH HARMONIC: The note is fretted normally and a harmonic is produced by adding the edge of the thumb or the tip of the index finger of the pick hand to the normal pick attack.

PICK SCRAPE: The edge of the pick is rubbed down (or up) the string, producing a scratchy sound.

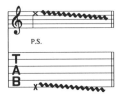

MUFFLED STRINGS: A percussive sound is produced by laying the fret hand across the string(s) without depressing, and striking them with the pick hand.

PALM MUTING: The note is partially muted by the pick hand lightly touching the string(s) just before the bridge.

RAKE: Drag the pick across the strings indicated with a single motion.

TREMOLO PICKING: The note is picked as rapidly and continuously as possible.

VIBRATO BAR DIVE AND RETURN: The pitch of the note or chord is dropped a specified number of steps (in rhythm) then returned to the original pitch.

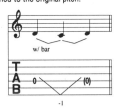

VIBRATO BAR SCOOP: Depress the bar just before striking the note, then quickly release the bar.

VIBRATO BAR DIP: Strike the note and then immediately drop a specified number of steps, then release back to the original pitch.